Contents

Your first hamster or gerbil

Hamsters and gerbils are lively little animals, and they love to play. Hamsters are nocturnal. This means that they like to sleep during the day and wake up at night.

▼ **Hamsters and gerbils are small and fragile.**

Hamsters and gerbils are very small and can easily get hurt. You should always be gentle when you are handling them.

4

Hamsters are nocturnal, and do not make good pets for young children as they tend to be asleep when the child wants to play. Hamsters and gerbils are easily hurt if they are dropped, so they may not be suitable pets for children who are boisterous. Children should always be supervised by an adult when they are playing with their hamster or gerbil.

Looking after an animal is your responsibility, not your child's. Before you buy one, try to make sure that he or she is not going to get bored with the hamster or gerbil.

▲ **Hamsters and gerbils usually live for between two to three years.**

5

Which pet?

Gerbils are very lively and do not like to be alone. It is best to buy two brothers or two sisters and keep them together.

**▲ Hamsters like
to live alone.**

Hamsters sleep during the day and wake up at night, so you will not be able to play with your hamster in the daytime. Do not mix gerbils and hamsters together.

**▼ Do not mix gerbils
and hamsters together.**

Lots of pets

There are many different **breeds** of hamster and gerbil. These have differently coloured fur and different markings.

◀ **Black Mongolian gerbil**

▶ **Agouti Syrian hamster**

▼ **Lilac Mongolian gerbil**

◄ Black Syrian hamster

► Albino gerbils

▲ Golden Satin Syrian hamster

Pet shopping list

Your hamster or gerbils will need:

A small cardboard box as a nest filled with shredded white kitchen towel, never use newspaper.

Or you could use hay...

...or wood shavings. Never use cedar or pine.

A cage or a plastic tank

▶ **Hamster food or gerbil food**

▲ **A scoop for cleaning out the tank**

◀ **A food bowl and a water bottle with a metal spout**

Your pet will enjoy some toys

Getting ready

The best home for a hamster or some gerbils is a plastic tank or a wire cage with a solid floor. It should be big enough for your pet to run around in.

Cover the floor with a layer of wood shavings. Add little piles of hay or shredded white kitchen towel so that your pet can make a cosy nest.

▲ **Gerbils will make a sleeping nest from the material you put in their tank.**

▲ **Make sure your hamster's tank or cage has a separate, nest box.**

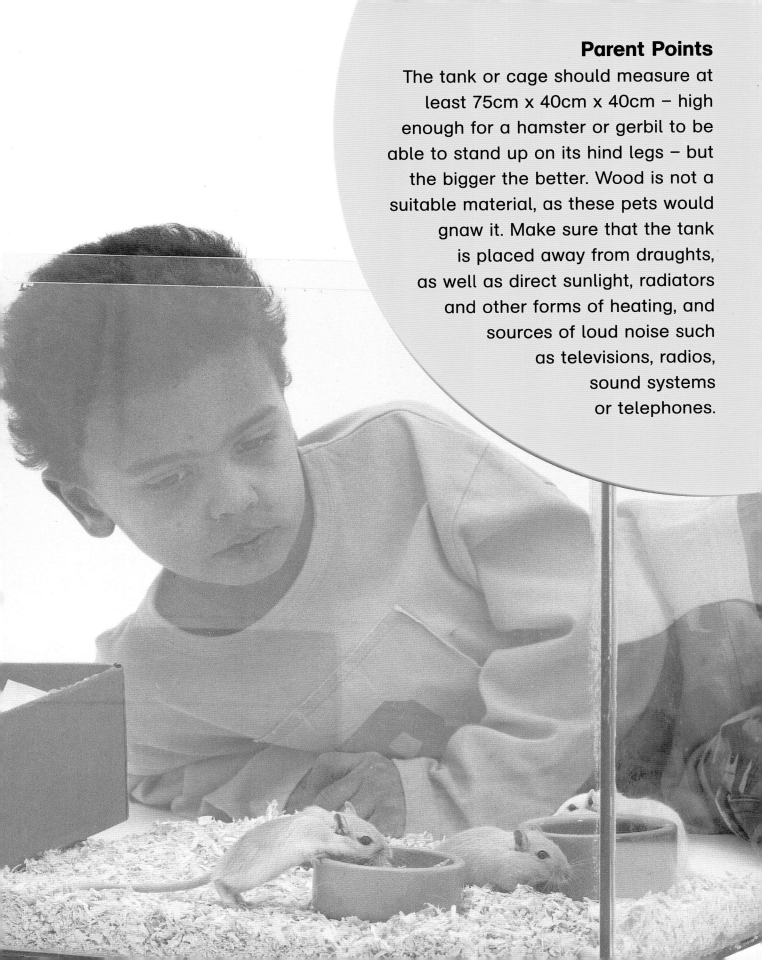

Saying hello

When your pet arrives, it may be feeling very scared. Place it gently in its tank or cage, and leave it alone for a couple of hours to get used to its new home.

Do not make any loud noises near it. Talk to it quietly, so that it begins to know your voice.

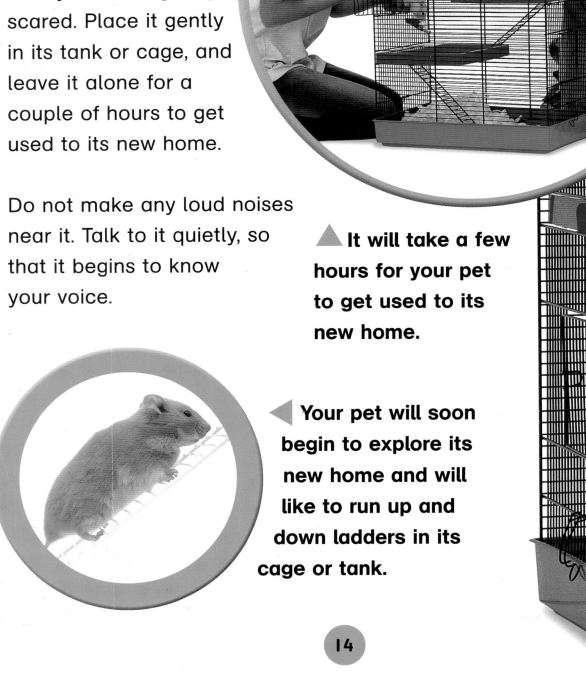

▲ **It will take a few hours for your pet to get used to its new home.**

◀ **Your pet will soon begin to explore its new home and will like to run up and down ladders in its cage or tank.**

You and Your Pet
Hamster
and Gerbil

Jean Coppendale

QED Publishing

First published in the UK in 2004 by
QED Publishing
A Quarto Group Company
226 City Road
London, EC1V 2TT

www.qed-publishing.co.uk

A Catalogue record for this book is available from the British Library.

ISBN 1 84538 288 9

Written by Jean Coppendale
Consultant Michaela Miller
Designed by Susi Martin
Editor Gill Munton
All photographs by Jane Burton except
page 18 (vegetables) by Chris Taylor
Picture of Cuddles on page 29 by Adelle Tracy
With many thanks to Adelle Tracey and Jumaane Bant
Creative Director Louise Morley
Editorial Manager Jean Coppendale

Printed and bound in China

Words in **bold** are
explained on page 32.

Handle with care

Hamsters and gerbils are very small, and a hand swooping down would scare them. Slowly put your closed hand into the tank or cage, and let your pet sniff it. Slowly open your hand, and let your pet climb onto your palm.

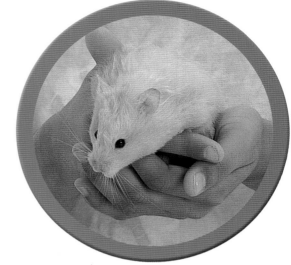

▲ **Always use two hands to hold your pet.**

◀ **To pick up your pet, gently scoop it into your palm. Never grab your pet around its body or dangle it by its tail.**

Offer your pet a treat, such as a piece of apple. After a couple of days your pet will begin to get used to you and let you cup it in your hand.

Parent Points
Make sure your child knows how to handle the hamster or gerbil before he or she tries to pick it up (see pages 16–17).

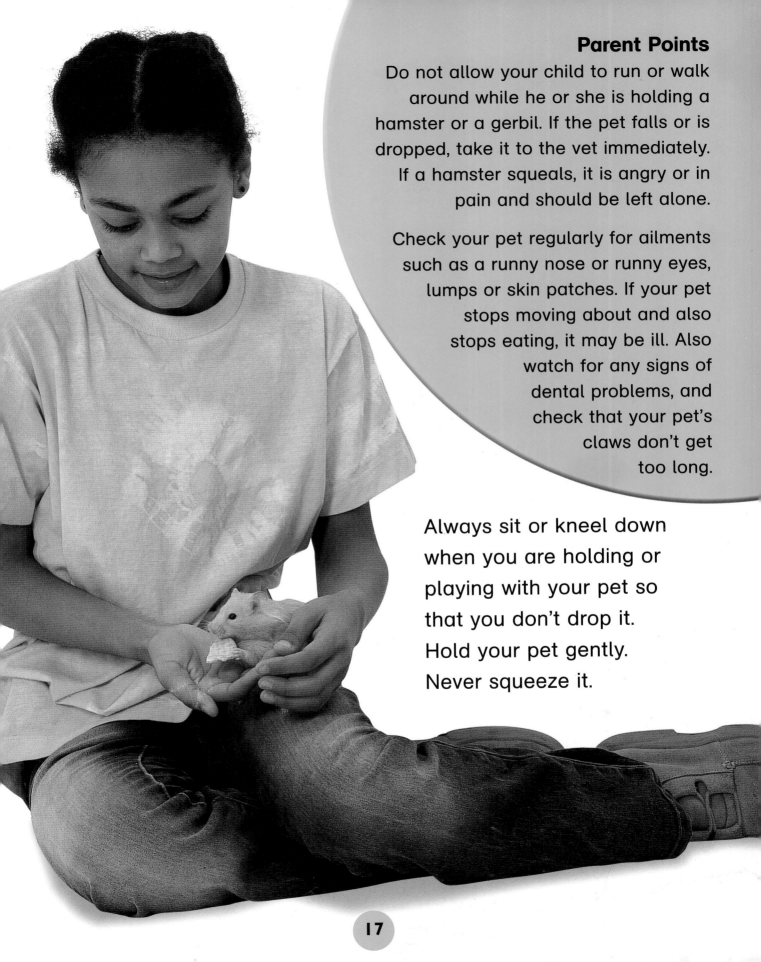

Always sit or kneel down when you are holding or playing with your pet so that you don't drop it. Hold your pet gently. Never squeeze it.

Feeding your pet

Your pet should always have some food. Buy special hamster or gerbil food from a pet shop or vet.

Carrot-shaped wood gnawing block

Feed your pet a piece of fresh fruit or vegetable every day. Try carrot, apple, celery, broccoli, banana or cucumber.

As a treat, hide a piece of plain biscuit or dry bread in the cage for your pet to find. Never give it sweets or sticky food.

Broccoli

Celery

Make sure your pet has a block of wood to gnaw on. This will help to keep its teeth short and healthy.

Make sure your pet's water bottle always has plenty of clean water in it.

Apple

Carrot

Parent Points
Do not feed hamsters and gerbils too much green food, as this can cause diarrhoea. Never change their diet suddenly; if you need to make a change, do so gradually over a few days. Do not feed either hamsters or gerbils acidic fruits such as oranges or strawberries.

Keep it clean

Your hamster's and gerbils' tank or cage needs to be kept clean. Give your hamster's home a really good clean every week. You should clean out your gerbil every two weeks.

▶ **Give the tank or cage a really good clean with a little animal-safe disinfectant. Wipe all the surfaces, and wash the toys.**

Once a day, use the scoop to clear out droppings and old bits of food.

Wash the food bowl every day. Clean out the water bottle with a bottle brush once a week.

Always wash your hands after you have cleaned out the tank.

Parent Points
Use animal-safe disinfectant (available from pet shops) for cleaning the tank. Make sure the pet is put somewhere safe while its home is being cleaned.

Your gerbil's life cycle

⑤

▶ When a female gerbil is about 9 weeks old, she can have babies. Her babies drink her milk. This is called suckling.

◀ At six weeks old, a gerbil is old enough to leave its mother.

④

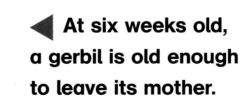

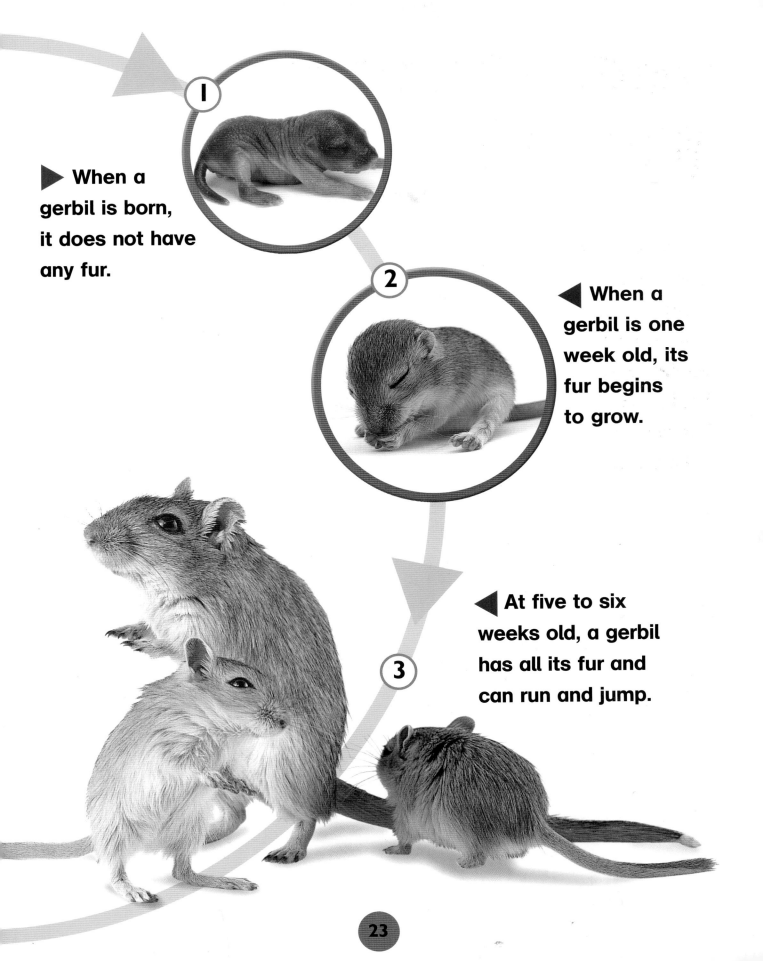

▶ When a gerbil is born, it does not have any fur.

◀ When a gerbil is one week old, its fur begins to grow.

◀ At five to six weeks old, a gerbil has all its fur and can run and jump.

Let's play!

Gerbils and hamsters are very active, so give your pet some toys. Put some cardboard tubes in the tank or cage. Cut holes in a plastic bottle for your pet to explore.

Hide some food for your pet to find.

▼ **Your pet will love to climb in and out of holes.**

 As a special treat, buy your pet a play tank. You'll enjoy watching it have fun.

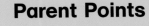 If you give your pet hamster a wheel, make sure it is a solid one, as its tail or legs may get trapped in an open wheel. Do not give a wheel to your pet gerbil.

Parent Points
Hamsters and gerbils should be allowed out of the tank or cage once a day, so that they can get some exercise. Make a playground in a large cardboard box with some toys. Make sure your pet cannot escape into corners, under doors, up chimneys, behind skirting boards or into pieces of furniture, and keep cats and dogs out of the room.

Make a

Make a playground for your pet to exercise in. Use an old cardboard box, old toilet roll tubes and old kitchen roll tubes and cartons.

playground

Saying goodbye

Pets grow older, just as people do. As your pet grows older, it will play less and spend more time sleeping. Don't give it as much food as before, or it will get fat.

My pet Cuddles

◀ **If your pet is ill, or appears to be in pain, take it to the vet.**

Cuddles last summer

Keep a special scrapbook about your pet

If your pet is very old or ill, it may die. Try not to be too sad, and remember all the fun you had.

You may want to bury your pet in the garden, or you can take it to the vet.

Pet checklist

Read this list, and think about all the points.

✔ **Hamsters and gerbils are not toys.**

✔ **Treat your pet gently – as you would like to be treated yourself.**

✔ **Gerbils and hamsters are very small and can be easily hurt if you are not gentle.**

✔ **How will you treat your pet if it makes you angry?**

✔ **Never shout at your pet, or frighten it.**

✔ **Animals feel pain, just as you do.**

✔ **Will you be happy to clean out your pet's cage or tank every day?**

Parents' checklist

- **You**, not your child, are responsible for the care of the pet.

- Your pet will need someone to look after it every day when you are away from home – this includes feeding, cleaning and exercising.

- Hamsters and gerbils are small pets, and can easily be stepped on – make sure your child is aware of the dangers.

- Exercise wheels are not suitable toys for gerbils as their tails can become trapped.

- Hamsters will bite if they are scared or angry.

- Hamsters should be left to sleep during the day. Don't keep two hamsters together, even if they are from the same litter.

- Never use newspaper in your pet's cage – it is poisonous to both hamsters and gerbils.

- Always supervise pets and children.

- If hamsters get too cold, they may go into hibernation and appear dead. Cup your hamster gently in your hands to warm it up.

Pet words

The fur of a hamster or gerbil is called its **coat**.

The long hairs on the face of a hamster or gerbil are called **whiskers**.

A gerbil has a long **tail**.

A hamster has hardly any **tail**.

Hamsters and gerbils have **claws** on their toes.

A **breed** is a special type of hamster or gerbil, such as a Black Mongolian gerbil or Black Syrian hamster.

Index

THE
OXFORD
Practical
ATLAS

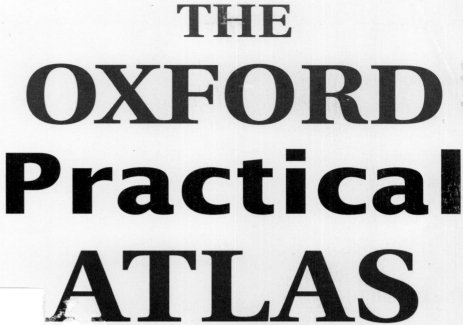

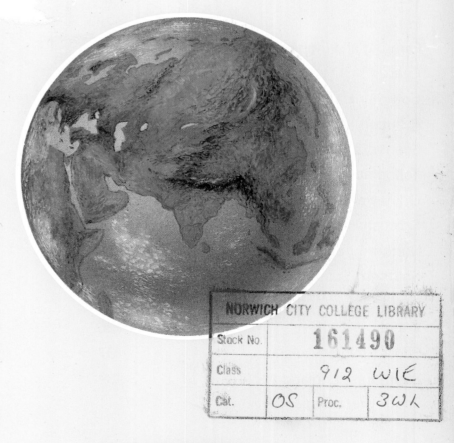

Acknowledgements

The publishers would like to thank the

Telegraph Colour Library
for permission to reproduce

Cover image:
Tom Van Sant / Geosphere Project, Santa Monica,
Science Photo Library.

The illustrations are by Chapman Bounford,
Hard Lines, and Gary Hinks.

The page design is by Adrian Smith.

Oil spillage data is from
*Oil Pollution Survey around the Coast
of the United Kingdom, 1995*
by kind permission of the publishers,
ACOPS (Advisory Committee on Protection of the Sea).

© Oxford University Press, 1997

© Maps copyright Oxford University Press

Oxford University Press, Great Clarendon Street, Oxford OX2 6DP

Oxford New York
Athens Auckland Bangkok Bombay
Calcutta Cape Town Dar es Salaam Delhi
Florence Hong Kong Istanbul Karachi
Kuala Lumpur Madras Madrid Melbourne
Mexico City Nairobi Paris Singapore
Taipei Tokyo Toronto

and associated companies in
Berlin Ibadan

Oxford is a trade mark of Oxford University Press

ISBN 0 19 831835 9 (paperback)   ISBN 0 19 831836 7 (hardback)

Printed in Italy by G. Canale & C. S.p.A. - Borgaro T.se - Turin

Editorial Adviser

Patrick Wiegand

Oxford University Press

2 **Contents** The World, The British Isles

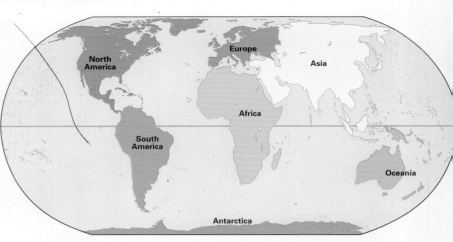

The World

The British Isles

Maps that show general features of regions, countries or continents are called **topographic maps.**
These maps are shown with a light band of colour in the contents list.

For example:

South West England

Key

CANADA Country name

Country area

A ALBANIA
AR ARMENIA
AU AUSTRIA
AZ AZERBAIJAN
B BELGIUM
BD BRUNEI DARUSSALAM
BE BENIN
BH BOSNIA-HERZEGOVINA
BU BURKINA
C CROATIA
CAR CENTRAL AFRICAN REPUBLIC
CZ CZECH REPUBLIC
G THE GAMBIA
G-B GUINEA-BISSAU
H HUNGARY
IS ISRAEL
L LEBANON
LI LITHUANIA
LU LUXEMBOURG
M FORMER YUGOSLAV
   REPUBLIC OF MACEDONIA
N NETHERLANDS
Q QATAR
R ROMANIA
S SLOVAKIA
SL SLOVENIA
SW SWITZERLAND
T TAJIKISTAN
TU TURKMENISTAN
U UGANDA
UAE UNITED ARAB EMIRATES
Y YUGOSLAVIA
ZIM ZIMBABWE

Scale

1: 105 000 000

One centimetre on the map represents
1050 kilometres on the ground.

0   1050   2100   3150   4200 km

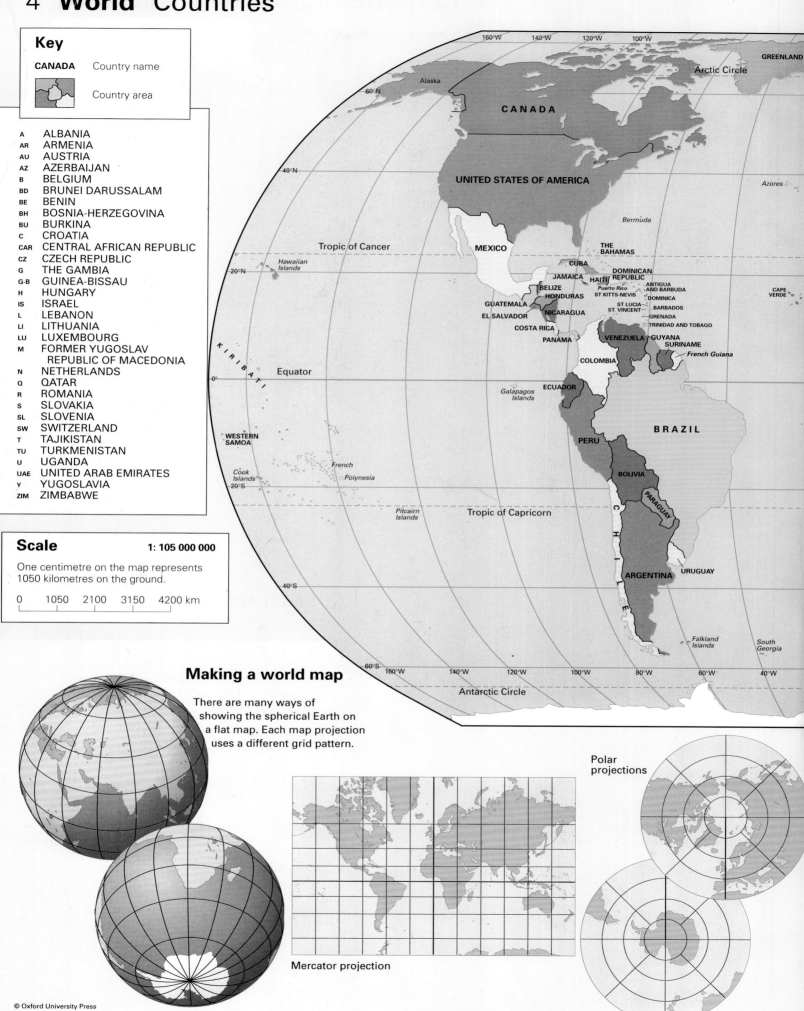

Making a world map

There are many ways of
showing the spherical Earth on
a flat map. Each map projection
uses a different grid pattern.

Polar
projections

Mercator projection

© Oxford University Press

Contents Continents and Poles 3

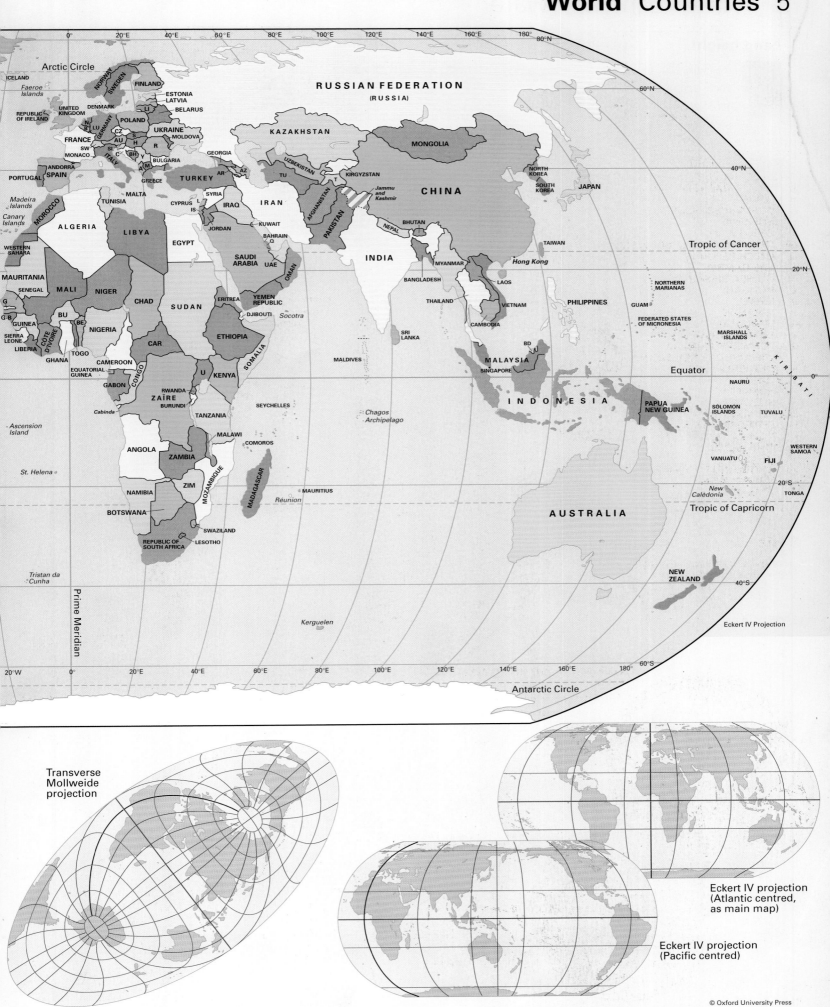

Arctic Circle

ICELAND
Faeroe Islands
REPUBLIC OF IRELAND
UNITED KINGDOM
PORTUGAL
Madeira Islands
Canary Islands
WESTERN SAHARA
MAURITANIA
SENEGAL
G
G-B
GUINEA
SIERRA LEONE
LIBERIA
COTE D'IVOIRE
GHANA
TOGO
EQUATORIAL GUINEA
GABON
St. Helena
Ascension Island
Tristan da Cunha

NORWAY
SWEDEN
FINLAND
DENMARK
ESTONIA
LATVIA
LI
BELARUS
N
B
LU
GERMANY
POLAND
CZ
UKRAINE
MOLDOVA
FRANCE
AU
S
H
R
MONACO
SW
C
BH
Y
ITALY
A
M
BULGARIA
ANDORRA
SPAIN
GREECE
TURKEY
AR
AZ
GEORGIA
MALTA
TUNISIA
CYPRUS
SYRIA
L
IS
IRAQ
IRAN
ALGERIA
LIBYA
EGYPT
JORDAN
KUWAIT
BAHRAIN
Q
SAUDI ARABIA
UAE
OMAN
MALI
NIGER
CHAD
SUDAN
ERITREA
YEMEN REPUBLIC
DJIBOUTI
Socotra
NIGERIA
CAR
ETHIOPIA
SOMALIA
BU
BE
CAMEROON
CONGO
U
KENYA
ZAIRE
RWANDA
BURUNDI
TANZANIA
SEYCHELLES
Cabinda
ANGOLA
ZAMBIA
MALAWI
COMOROS
Chagos Archipelago
NAMIBIA
ZIM
MOZAMBIQUE
MADAGASCAR
MAURITIUS
Réunion
BOTSWANA
SWAZILAND
REPUBLIC OF SOUTH AFRICA
LESOTHO

RUSSIAN FEDERATION
(RUSSIA)

KAZAKHSTAN
MONGOLIA
UZBEKISTAN
TU
KIRGYZSTAN
T
AFGHANISTAN
PAKISTAN
Jammu and Kashmir
CHINA
NEPAL
BHUTAN
INDIA
MYANMAR
BANGLADESH
LAOS
THAILAND
VIETNAM
CAMBODIA
SRI LANKA
MALDIVES
MALAYSIA
SINGAPORE
INDONESIA

NORTH KOREA
SOUTH KOREA
JAPAN
TAIWAN
Hong Kong
PHILIPPINES
GUAM
NORTHERN MARIANAS
FEDERATED STATES OF MICRONESIA
MARSHALL ISLANDS
PAPUA NEW GUINEA
SOLOMON ISLANDS
NAURU
TUVALU
KIRIBATI
VANUATU
New Caledonia
FIJI
WESTERN SAMOA
TONGA

AUSTRALIA

NEW ZEALAND

Tropic of Cancer
Equator
Tropic of Capricorn

Prime Meridian

80°N
60°N
40°N
20°N
0°
20°S
40°S
60°S

0° 20°E 40°E 60°E 80°E 100°E 120°E 140°E 160°E 180°

20°W 0° 20°E 40°E 60°E 80°E 100°E 120°E 140°E 160°E 180°

Kerguelen

Eckert IV Projection

Antarctic Circle

Transverse Mollweide projection

Eckert IV projection (Atlantic centred, as main map)

Eckert IV projection (Pacific centred)

© Oxford University Press

Land height

- more than 5000 m
- 2000 - 5000 m
- 1000 - 2000 m
- 500 - 1000 m
- 200 - 500 m
- 0 - 200 m
- below sea level
- ▲ peak or highest point

Sea depth

- 0 - 200 m
- 200 - 4000 m
- 4000 - 7000 m
- more than 7000 m

Scale

1: 105 000 000

One centimetre on the map represents
1050 kilometres on the ground
at the Equator.

| 0 | 1050 | 2100 | 3150 | 4200 km |

high mountains

peak or
highest point

hills

plains

continental
shelf

ocean basin

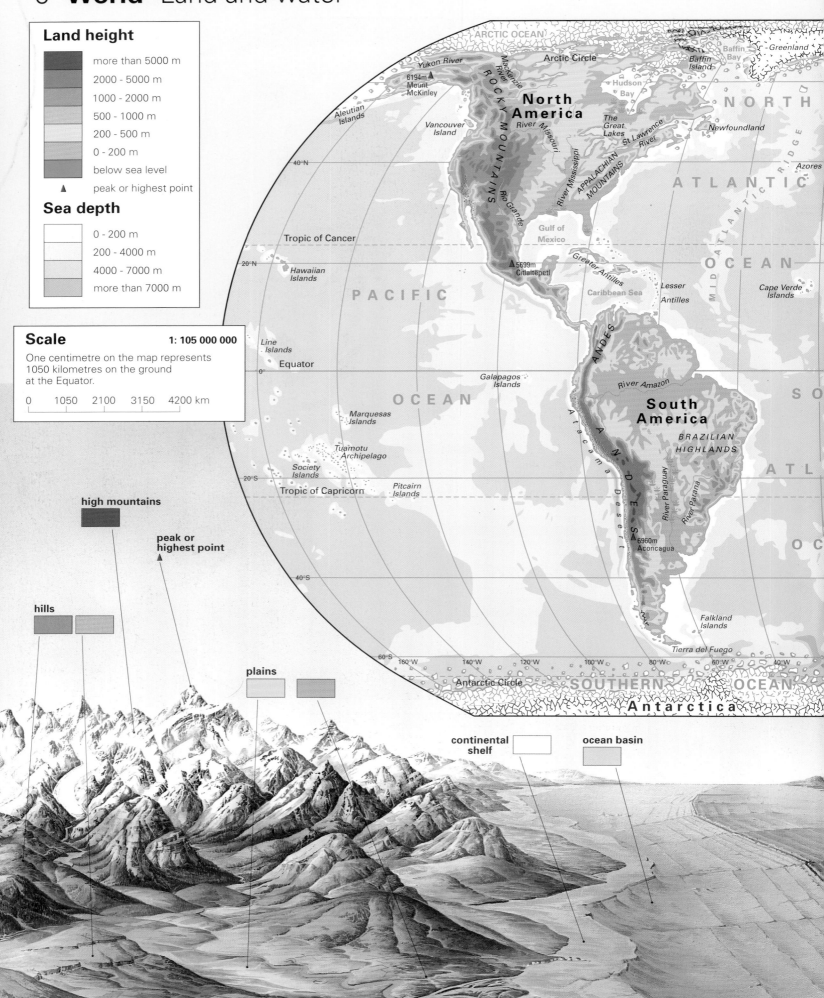

ARCTIC OCEAN
Greenland
Arctic Circle
Baffin Bay
Baffin Island
Yukon River
Mackenzie River
6194m Mount McKinley
ROCKY MOUNTAINS
Hudson Bay
Aleutian Islands
Vancouver Island
North America
River Missouri
The Great Lakes
St Lawrence River
Newfoundland
NORTH
40°N
River Mississippi
APPALACHIAN MOUNTAINS
ATLANTIC
Azores
MID ATLANTIC RIDGE
Rio Grande
Tropic of Cancer
Gulf of Mexico
OCEAN
20°N
PACIFIC
Hawaiian Islands
5699m Citlaltépetl
Greater Antilles
Caribbean Sea
Lesser Antilles
Cape Verde Islands
Line Islands
OCEAN
Equator
Galapagos Islands
ANDES
South America
BRAZILIAN HIGHLANDS
SO
Marquesas Islands
River Amazon
ATL
Tuamotu Archipelago
Society Islands
20°S
River Paraguay
River Parana
Pitcairn Islands
Tropic of Capricorn
Atacama Desert
OC
6960m Aconcagua
40°S
Falkland Islands
Tierra del Fuego
60°S 160°W 140°W 120°W 100°W 80°W 60°W 40°W
Antarctic Circle
SOUTHERN OCEAN
Antarctica

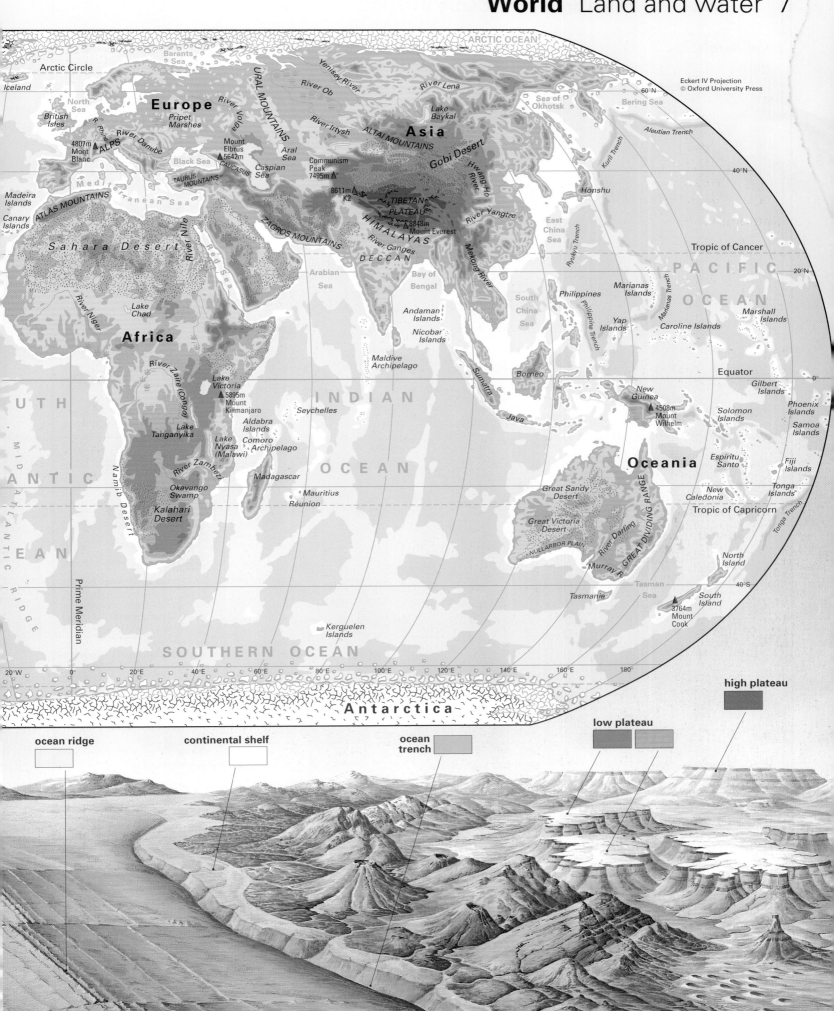

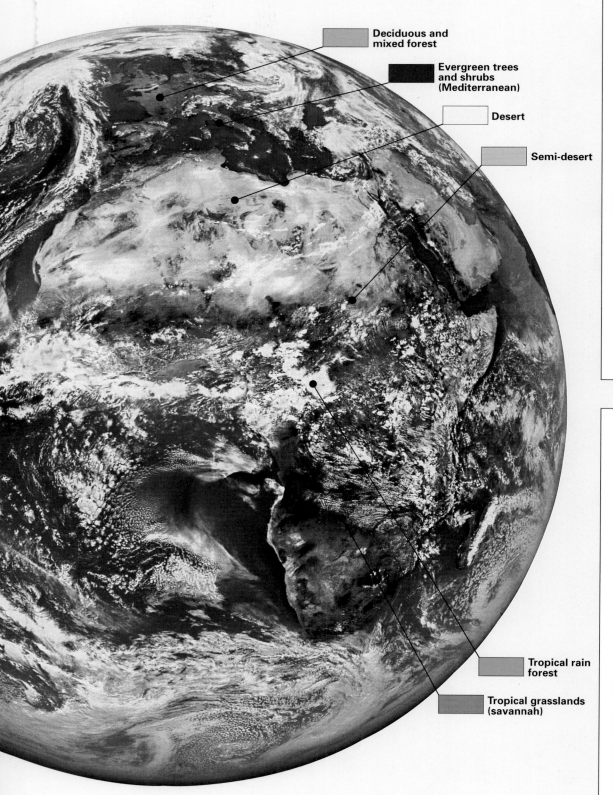

Deciduous and
mixed forest

Evergreen trees
and shrubs
(Mediterranean)

Desert

Semi-desert

Tropical rain
forest

Tropical grasslands
(savannah)

A Meteosat view of
the Earth recorded
by a geostationary satellite
positioned 36 000 km above
the intersection of the
Prime Meridian and the Equator

Climatic regions

Hot tropical rainy

rain all year

monsoon

dry in winter

Very dry

with no reliable rain

with a little rain

**Influenced by the sea:
warm summers, mild winters**

with dry summers
(Mediterranean type)

with dry winters

with no dry season

Cool

with dry winters

rain all year

Cold polar

no warm season
and fairly dry

Mountain

height of the land strongly
affects the climate

Ecosystems

Vegetation types are those which
would occur naturally without
interference by people

Coniferous forest

cone bearing trees

Deciduous and mixed forest

leaf shedding and
coniferous tress

Tropical rain forest

many species of lush,
tall trees

Tropical grasslands (savannah)

tall grass parkland
with scattered trees

Thorn forest

low trees and shrubs with
spines or thorns

Evergreen trees and shrubs

plants and small trees
with leathery leaves

Temperate grasslands

prairies,steppes,
pampas and veld

Semi-desert

short grasses and
drought-resistant scrub

Desert

sand and stones,
very little vegetation

Tundra

moss and lichen,
with few trees

Ice

no vegetation

Mountains

thin soils, steep slopes
and high altitude affects
type of vegetation

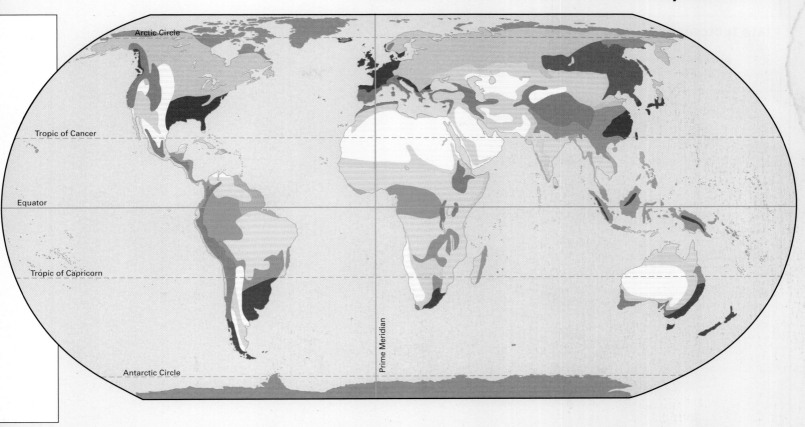

Arctic Circle

Tropic of Cancer

Equator

Tropic of Capricorn

Prime Meridian

Antarctic Circle

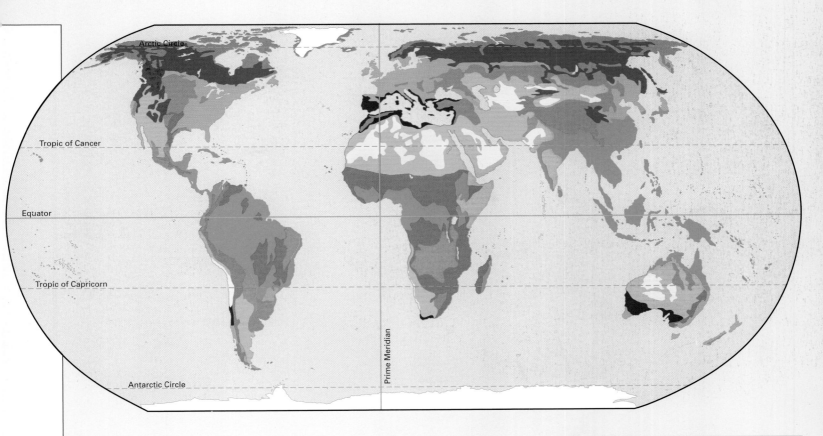

Arctic Circle

Tropic of Cancer

Equator

Tropic of Capricorn

Prime Meridian

Antarctic Circle

Scale 1: 190 000 000

One centimetre on the map represents
1900 kilometres on the ground
at the Equator.

0 1900 3800 5700 km

Eckert IV Projection

© Oxford University Press

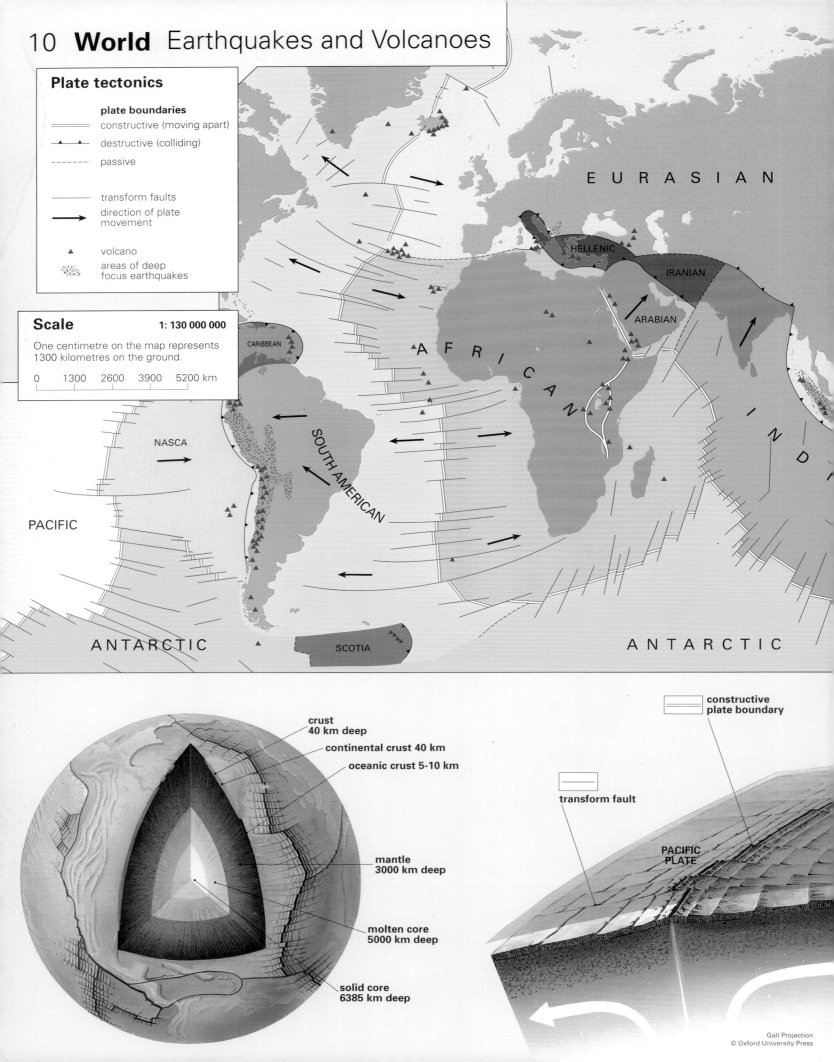

Plate tectonics

plate boundaries

constructive (moving apart)

destructive (colliding)

passive

transform faults

direction of plate
movement

▲ volcano

areas of deep
focus earthquakes

Scale   1: 130 000 000

One centimetre on the map represents
1300 kilometres on the ground.

0   1300   2600   3900   5200 km

EURASIAN

HELLENIC

IRANIAN

ARABIAN

AFRICAN

CARIBBEAN

NASCA

SOUTH AMERICAN

PACIFIC

INDI

ANTARCTIC

SCOTIA

ANTARCTIC

crust
40 km deep

continental crust 40 km

oceanic crust 5-10 km

mantle
3000 km deep

molten core
5000 km deep

solid core
6385 km deep

constructive
plate boundary

transform fault

PACIFIC
PLATE

Gall Projection
© Oxford University Press

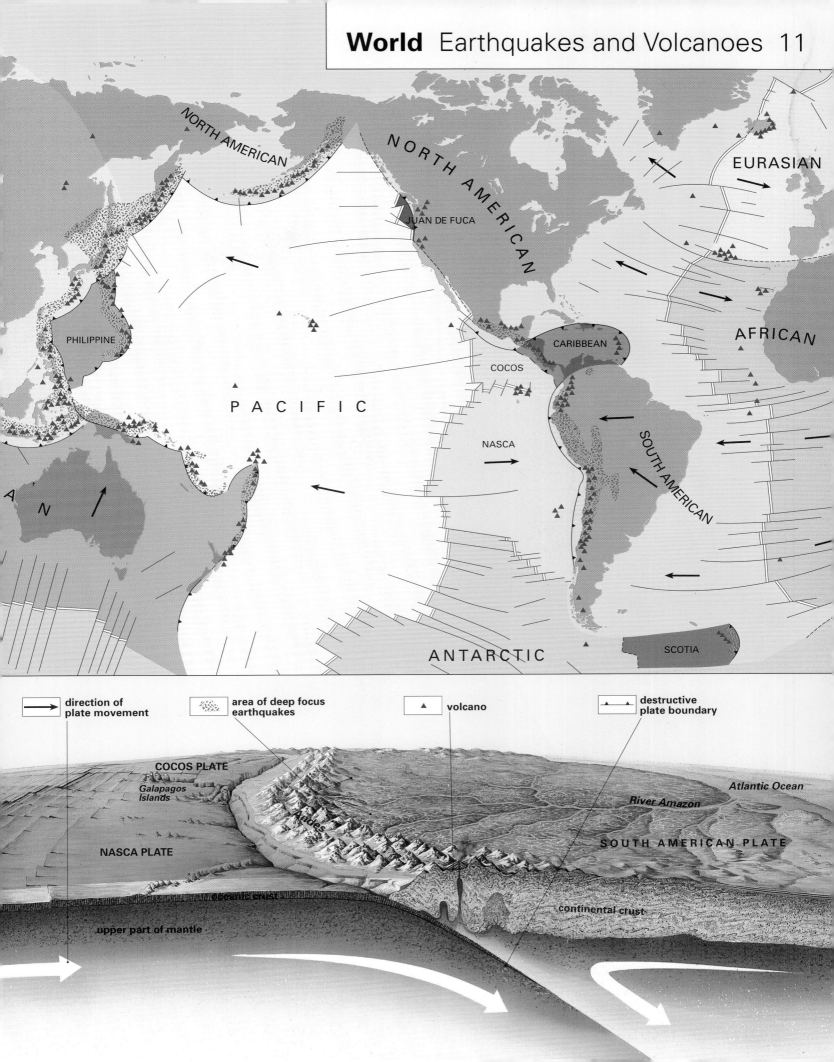

NORTH AMERICAN

NORTH AMERICAN

EURASIAN

JUAN DE FUCA

AFRICAN

PHILIPPINE

CARIBBEAN

COCOS

PACIFIC

NASCA

SOUTH AMERICAN

N

ANTARCTIC

SCOTIA

| → | direction of plate movement | | area of deep focus earthquakes | ▲ | volcano | | destructive plate boundary |

COCOS PLATE

Galapagos Islands

Atlantic Ocean

River Amazon

SOUTH AMERICAN PLATE

Andes

NASCA PLATE

oceanic crust

continental crust

upper part of mantle

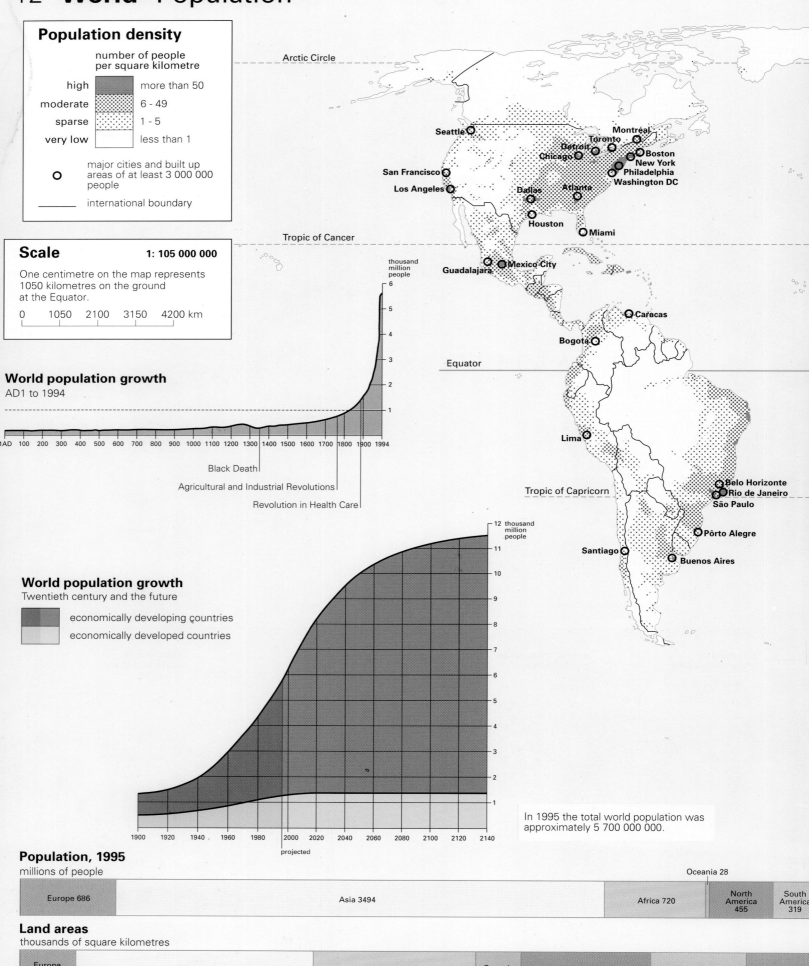

Population density

number of people per square kilometre

high		more than 50
moderate		6 - 49
sparse		1 - 5
very low		less than 1

○ major cities and built up areas of at least 3 000 000 people

─── international boundary

Scale

1: 105 000 000

One centimetre on the map represents 1050 kilometres on the ground at the Equator.

0   1050   2100   3150   4200 km

World population growth

AD1 to 1994

Black Death

Agricultural and Industrial Revolutions

Revolution in Health Care

World population growth

Twentieth century and the future

- economically developing countries
- economically developed countries

In 1995 the total world population was approximately 5 700 000 000.

Population, 1995

millions of people

| Europe 686 | Asia 3494 | Africa 720 | North America 455 | South America 319 |

Oceania 28

Land areas

thousands of square kilometres

| Europe 10 498 | Asia 44 387 | Africa 30 335 | Oceania 8503 | North America 24 241 | South America 17 832 | Antarctica 13 340 |

Arctic Circle

Seattle · Montréal · Toronto · Detroit · Boston · Chicago · New York · Philadelphia · Washington DC · San Francisco · Los Angeles · Dallas · Atlanta · Houston · Miami

Tropic of Cancer

Guadalajara · Mexico City · Caracas · Bogotá

Equator

Lima

Belo Horizonte · Rio de Janeiro · São Paulo

Tropic of Capricorn

Pôrto Alegre · Santiago · Buenos Aires

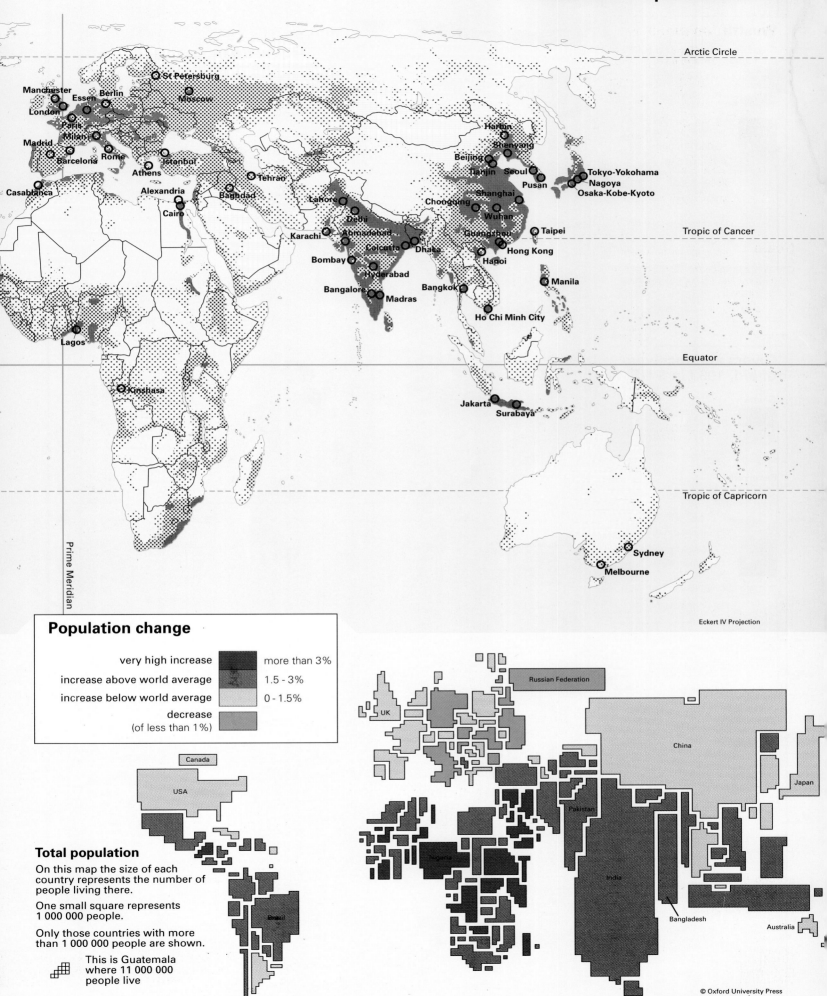

Arctic Circle

St Petersburg

Manchester
Essen Berlin
London
Paris
Madrid Milan
Barcelona Rome
Casablanca
Athens
Istanbul
Tehran

Moscow

Harbin
Shenyang
Beijing
Tianjin Seoul
Pusan
Shanghai

Tokyo-Yokohama
Nagoya
Osaka-Kobe-Kyoto

Chongqing

Alexandria
Baghdad
Cairo

Lahore
Delhi
Karachi Ahmadabad
Bombay Calcutta Dhaka
Hyderabad
Bangalore Madras

Wuhan

Guangzhou
Hanoi
Hong Kong

Taipei

Tropic of Cancer

Bangkok

Manila

Ho Chi Minh City

Lagos

Equator

Kinshasa

Jakarta
Surabaya

Tropic of Capricorn

Eckert IV Projection

Sydney
Melbourne

Prime Meridian

Population change

very high increase		more than 3%
increase above world average		1.5 - 3%
increase below world average		0 - 1.5%
decrease (of less than 1%)		

Russian Federation

UK

China

Japan

Canada

USA

Total population

On this map the size of each country represents the number of people living there.

One small square represents 1 000 000 people.

Only those countries with more than 1 000 000 people are shown.

This is Guatemala where 11 000 000 people live

Nigeria

Pakistan

India

Bangladesh

Australia

Brazil

© Oxford University Press

Wealth

Gross Domestic Product (GDP) per person, 1992 in $ US

The annual total value of all the goods and services produced in a country, divided by the number of people living in that country.

15 000–24 000 (the top 25 in the world)

10 000–15 000

5000–10 000
— World average

3000–5000

1000–3000

under 1000 (the bottom 22 in the world)

—— international boundary

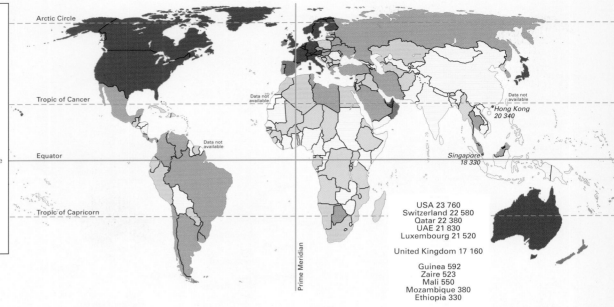

Data not available

Hong Kong 20 340

Singapore 18 330

USA 23 760
Switzerland 22 580
Qatar 22 380
UAE 21 830
Luxembourg 21 520

United Kingdom 17 160

Guinea 592
Zaire 523
Mali 550
Mozambique 380
Ethiopia 330

Givers and receivers of aid, 1993 in $ US

Givers

more than 100 per person

50-100 per person

25-50 per person

Receivers

0-10 per person

10-25 per person

25-50 per person

50-100 per person

more than 100 per person

—— international boundary

data not available

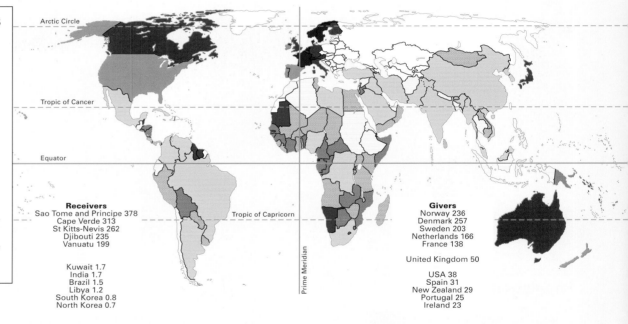

Receivers
Sao Tome and Principe 378
Cape Verde 313
St Kitts-Nevis 262
Djibouti 235
Vanuatu 199

Kuwait 1.7
India 1.7
Brazil 1.5
Libya 1.2
South Korea 0.8
North Korea 0.7

Givers
Norway 236
Denmark 257
Sweden 203
Netherlands 166
France 138

United Kingdom 50

USA 38
Spain 31
New Zealand 29
Portugal 25
Ireland 23

Life expectancy

Average number of years a baby

70 years and over

65-70 years

55-65 years

45-55 years

35-45 years

—— international boundary

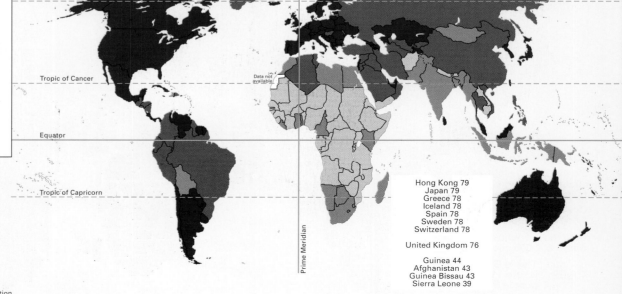

Data not available

Hong Kong 79
Japan 79
Greece 78
Iceland 78
Spain 78
Sweden 78
Switzerland 78

United Kingdom 76

Guinea 44
Afghanistan 43
Guinea Bissau 43
Sierra Leone 39

Scale   1: 235 000 000

One centimetre on the map represents 2350 kilometres on the ground at the Equator.

0   2350   4700   7050 km

    Eckert IV Projection

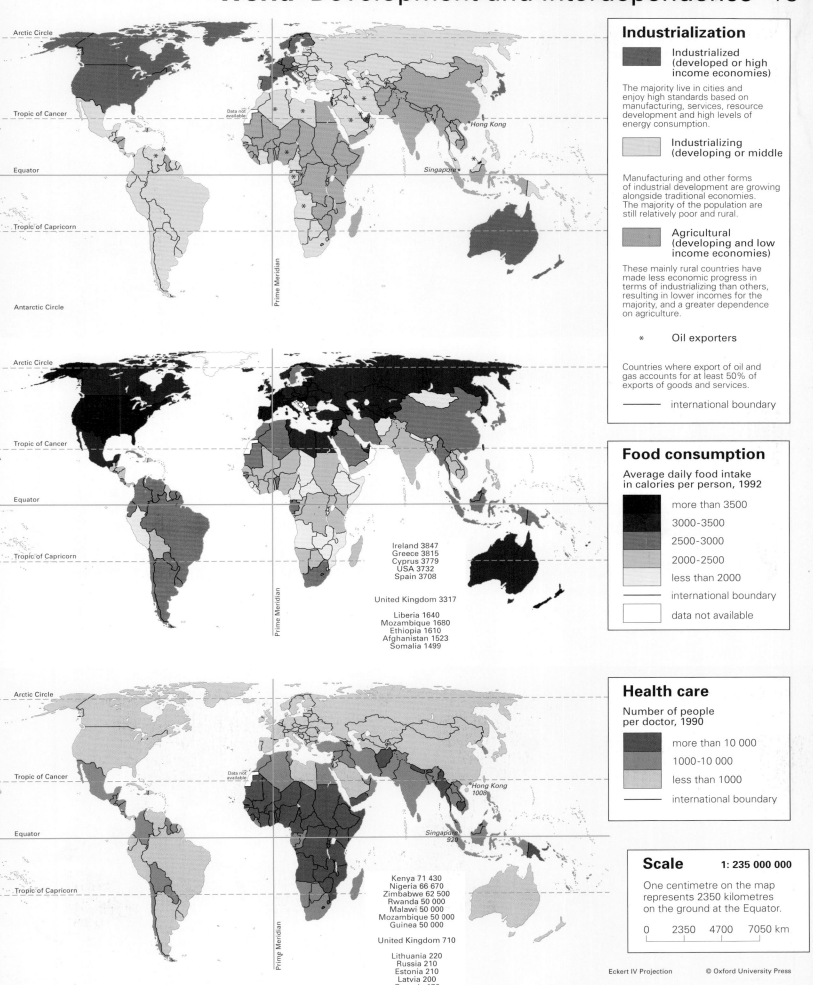

Industrialization

Industrialized (developed or high income economies)

The majority live in cities and enjoy high standards based on manufacturing, services, resource development and high levels of energy consumption.

Industrializing (developing or middle

Manufacturing and other forms of industrial development are growing alongside traditional economies. The majority of the population are still relatively poor and rural.

Agricultural (developing and low income economies)

These mainly rural countries have made less economic progress in terms of industrializing than others, resulting in lower incomes for the majority, and a greater dependence on agriculture.

* **Oil exporters**

Countries where export of oil and gas accounts for at least 50% of exports of goods and services.

—— international boundary

Hong Kong

Data not available

Singapore •

Food consumption

Average daily food intake in calories per person, 1992

more than 3500
3000-3500
2500-3000
2000-2500
less than 2000
—— international boundary
data not available

Ireland 3847
Greece 3815
Cyprus 3779
USA 3732
Spain 3708

United Kingdom 3317

Liberia 1640
Mozambique 1680
Ethiopia 1610
Afghanistan 1523
Somalia 1499

Health care

Number of people per doctor, 1990

more than 10 000
1000-10 000
less than 1000
—— international boundary

Hong Kong 1008

Singapore 920

Kenya 71 430
Nigeria 66 670
Zimbabwe 62 500
Rwanda 50 000
Malawi 50 000
Mozambique 50 000
Guinea 50 000

United Kingdom 710

Lithuania 220
Russia 210
Estonia 210
Latvia 200
Georgia 170

Scale   1: 235 000 000

One centimetre on the map represents 2350 kilometres on the ground at the Equator.

0   2350   4700   7050 km

Eckert IV Projection   © Oxford University Press

Arctic Circle
Tropic of Cancer
Equator
Tropic of Capricorn
Antarctic Circle
Prime Meridian

Water

Surplus

Enough water to support
vegetation and crops
without irrigation

large surplus

surplus

Deficiency

Not enough water to support
vegetation and crops without
irrigation. After long periods of
deficiency, these areas may lose
their natural vegetation.

deficiency

chronic deficiency

international boundary

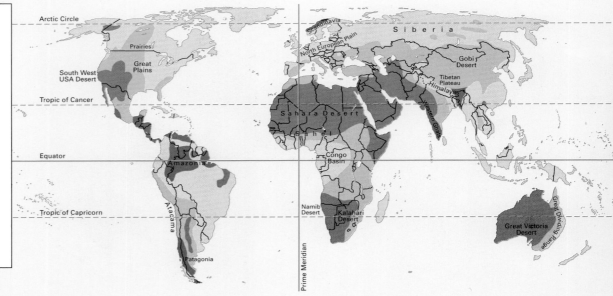

Desertification

existing areas of desert

areas with a high risk of desertification

areas with a moderate risk of desertification

international boundary

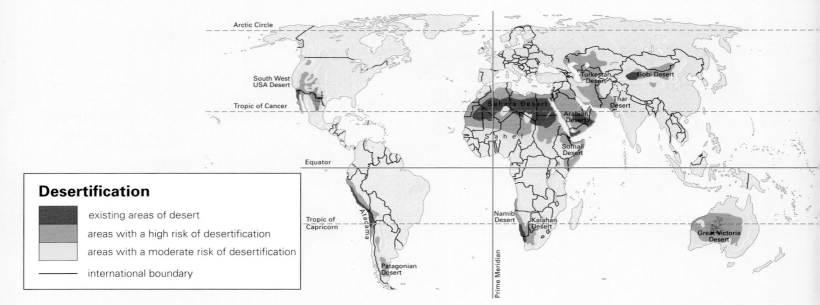

Tropical deforestation

existing areas of rainforest

former areas of rainforest

international boundary

Scale   1: 235 000 000

One centimetre on the map
measures 2350 kilometres
on the ground at the Equator.

0   2350   4700   7050 km

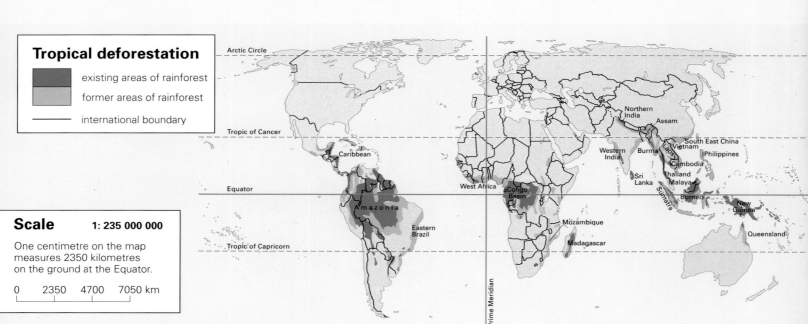

Eckert IV Projection

© Oxford University Press

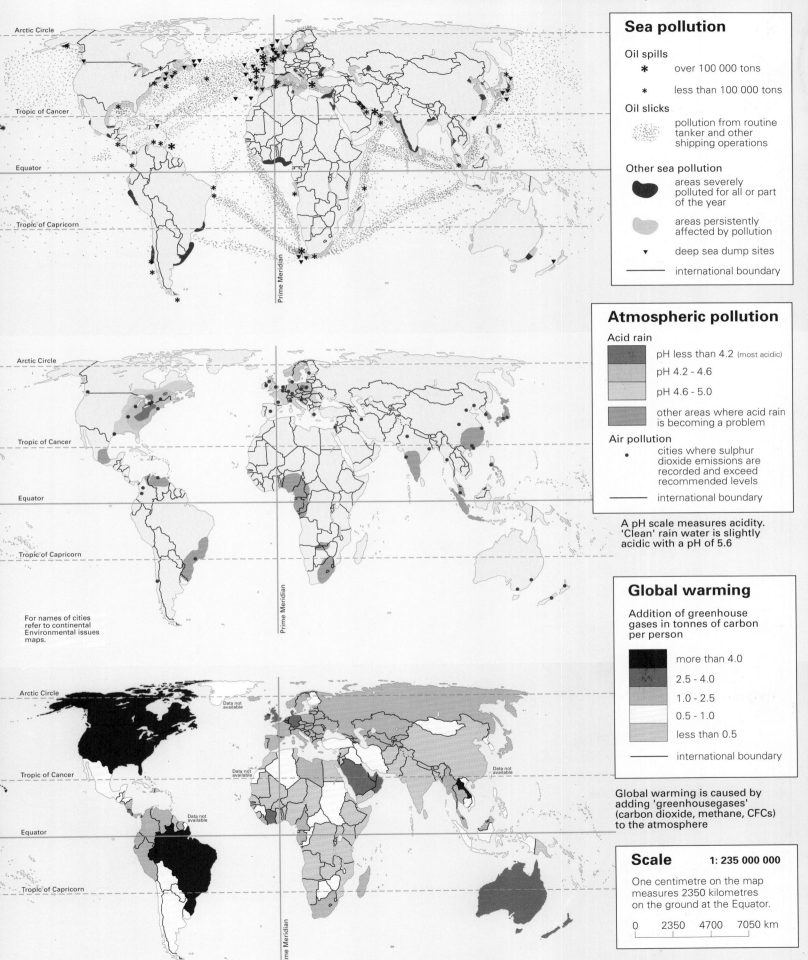

Sea pollution

Oil spills

| ⁂ | over 100 000 tons |
| ✳ | less than 100 000 tons |

Oil slicks

pollution from routine tanker and other shipping operations

Other sea pollution

areas severely polluted for all or part of the year

areas persistently affected by pollution

▼ deep sea dump sites

international boundary

Atmospheric pollution

Acid rain

pH less than 4.2 (most acidic)

pH 4.2 - 4.6

pH 4.6 - 5.0

other areas where acid rain is becoming a problem

Air pollution

• cities where sulphur dioxide emissions are recorded and exceed recommended levels

international boundary

A pH scale measures acidity. 'Clean' rain water is slightly acidic with a pH of 5.6

Global warming

Addition of greenhouse gases in tonnes of carbon per person

more than 4.0

2.5 - 4.0

1.0 - 2.5

0.5 - 1.0

less than 0.5

international boundary

Global warming is caused by adding 'greenhousegases' (carbon dioxide, methane, CFCs) to the atmosphere

Scale   1: 235 000 000

One centimetre on the map measures 2350 kilometres on the ground at the Equator.

0   2350   4700   7050 km

For names of cities refer to continental Environmental issues maps.

Eckert IV Projection

© Oxford University Press

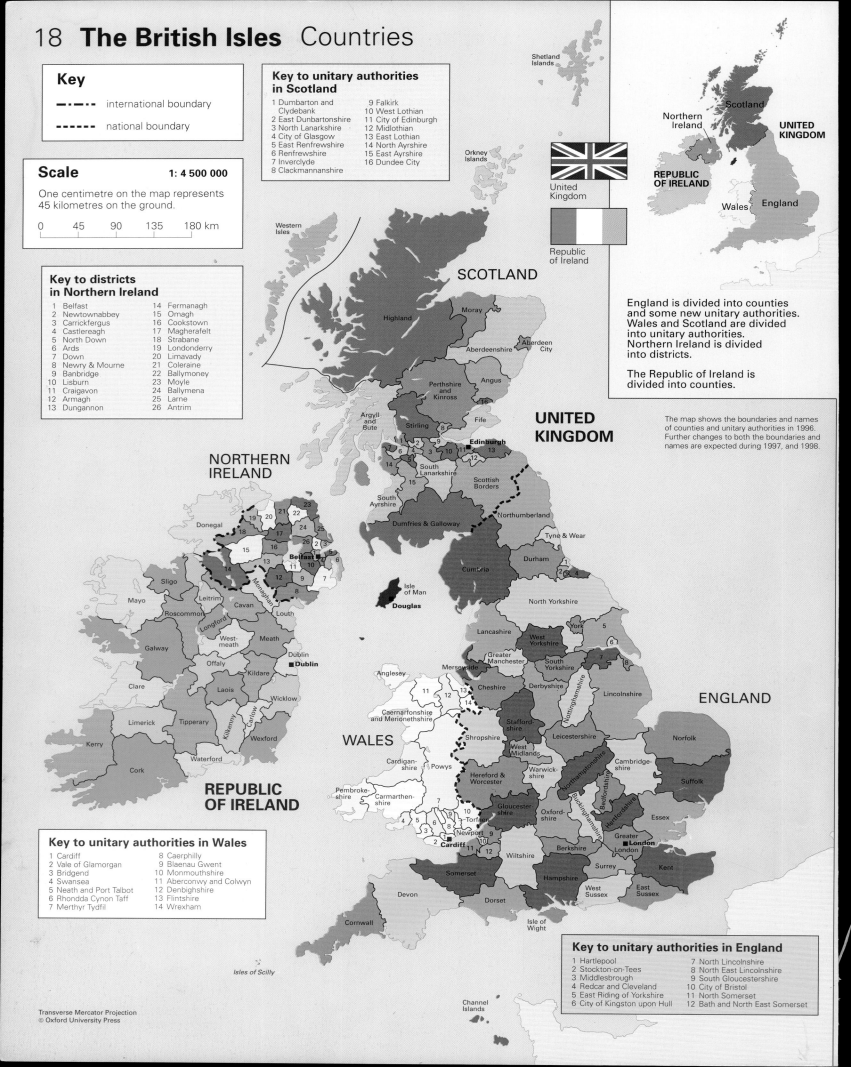

Key

—·—·—·— international boundary

------ national boundary

Scale
1: 4 500 000

One centimetre on the map represents
45 kilometres on the ground.

0   45   90   135   180 km

Key to unitary authorities in Scotland

1 Dumbarton and Clydebank
2 East Dunbartonshire
3 North Lanarkshire
4 City of Glasgow
5 East Renfrewshire
6 Renfrewshire
7 Inverclyde
8 Clackmannanshire
9 Falkirk
10 West Lothian
11 City of Edinburgh
12 Midlothian
13 East Lothian
14 North Ayrshire
15 East Ayrshire
16 Dundee City

Key to districts in Northern Ireland

1 Belfast
2 Newtownabbey
3 Carrickfergus
4 Castlereagh
5 North Down
6 Ards
7 Down
8 Newry & Mourne
9 Banbridge
10 Lisburn
11 Craigavon
12 Armagh
13 Dungannon
14 Fermanagh
15 Omagh
16 Cookstown
17 Magherafelt
18 Strabane
19 Londonderry
20 Limavady
21 Coleraine
22 Ballymoney
23 Moyle
24 Ballymena
25 Larne
26 Antrim

Key to unitary authorities in Wales

1 Cardiff
2 Vale of Glamorgan
3 Bridgend
4 Swansea
5 Neath and Port Talbot
6 Rhondda Cynon Taff
7 Merthyr Tydfil
8 Caerphilly
9 Blaenau Gwent
10 Monmouthshire
11 Aberconwy and Colwyn
12 Denbighshire
13 Flintshire
14 Wrexham

Key to unitary authorities in England

1 Hartlepool
2 Stockton-on-Tees
3 Middlesbrough
4 Redcar and Cleveland
5 East Riding of Yorkshire
6 City of Kingston upon Hull
7 North Lincolnshire
8 North East Lincolnshire
9 South Gloucestershire
10 City of Bristol
11 North Somerset
12 Bath and North East Somerset

England is divided into counties
and some new unitary authorities.
Wales and Scotland are divided
into unitary authorities.
Northern Ireland is divided
into districts.

The Republic of Ireland is
divided into counties.

The map shows the boundaries and names
of counties and unitary authorities in 1996.
Further changes to both the boundaries and
names are expected during 1997, and 1998.

United Kingdom

Republic of Ireland

UNITED KINGDOM

REPUBLIC OF IRELAND

Northern Ireland

Scotland

Wales

England

Transverse Mercator Projection
© Oxford University Press

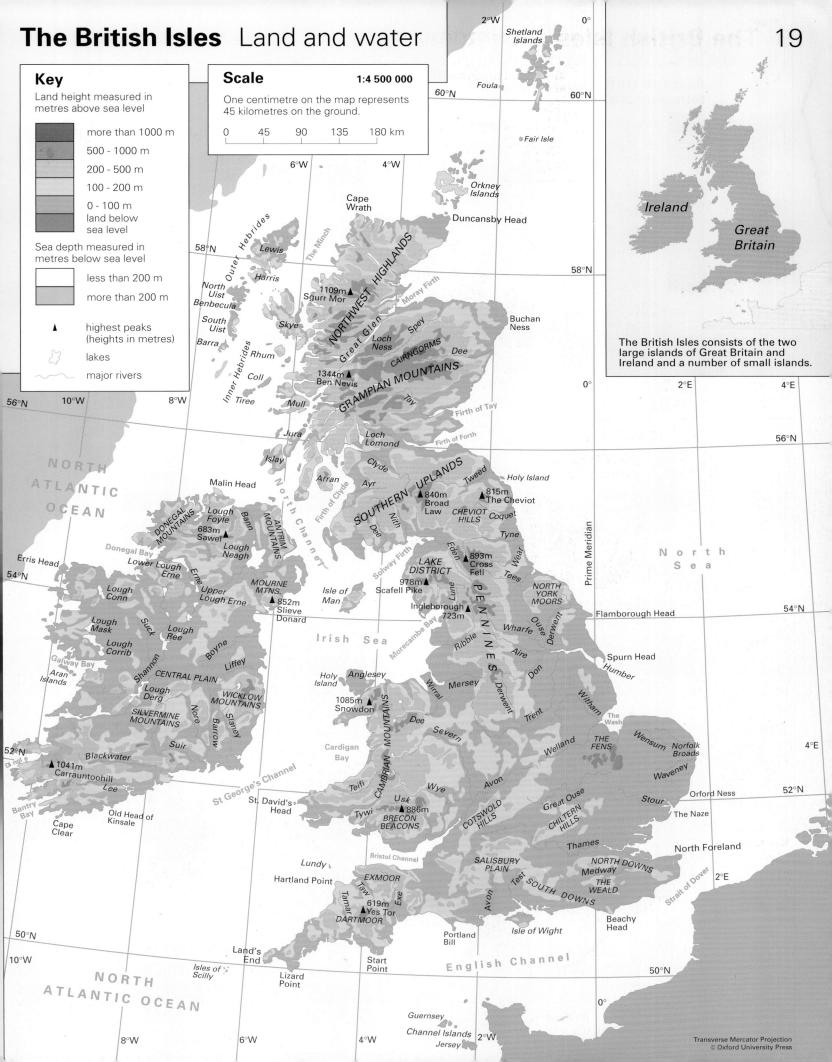

Key

Land height measured in metres above sea level

- more than 1000 m
- 500 - 1000 m
- 200 - 500 m
- 100 - 200 m
- 0 - 100 m
- land below sea level

Sea depth measured in metres below sea level

- less than 200 m
- more than 200 m

▲ highest peaks (heights in metres)

lakes

major rivers

Scale

1:4 500 000

One centimetre on the map represents 45 kilometres on the ground.

0   45   90   135   180 km

The British Isles consists of the two large islands of Great Britain and Ireland and a number of small islands.

Transverse Mercator Projection
© Oxford University Press

Average surface temperature

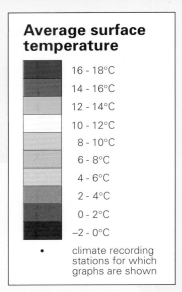

- 16 - 18°C
- 14 - 16°C
- 12 - 14°C
- 10 - 12°C
- 8 - 10°C
- 6 - 8°C
- 4 - 6°C
- 2 - 4°C
- 0 - 2°C
- −2 - 0°C

• climate recording stations for which graphs are shown

Scale

1: 8 000 000

One centimetre on the map represents 80 kilometres on the ground.

0   80   160   240 km

January temperature

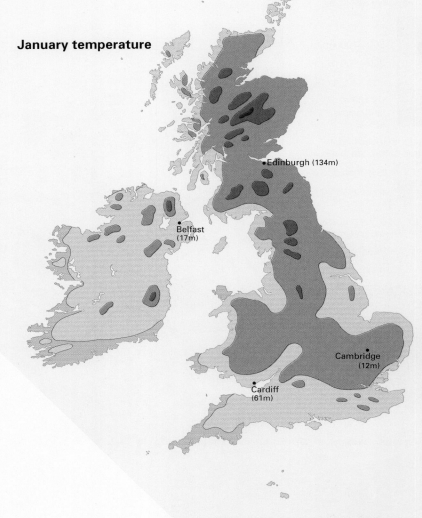

•Edinburgh (134m)

•Belfast (17m)

Cambridge (12m)

Cardiff (61m)

July temperature

Edinburgh (134m)

•Belfast (17m)

Cambridge (12m)

Cardiff (61m)

Transverse Mercator Projection
© Oxford University Press

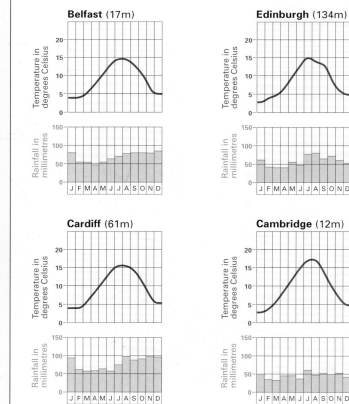

Belfast (17m)

Edinburgh (134m)

Cardiff (61m)

Cambridge (12m)

Temperature in degrees Celsius

Rainfall in millimetres

J F M A M J J A S O N D

Average annual rainfall

- more than 2400 millimetres
- 1200 - 2400 millimetres
- 800 - 1200 millimetres
- less than 800 millimetres
- • climate recording stations for which graphs are shown

Drought and flood

- inland areas in regular danger of flooding
- coastal areas in regular danger of flooding
- areas in regular danger of drought

Scale   1: 8 000 000

One centimetre on the map measures 80 kilometres on the ground.

0   80   160   240 km

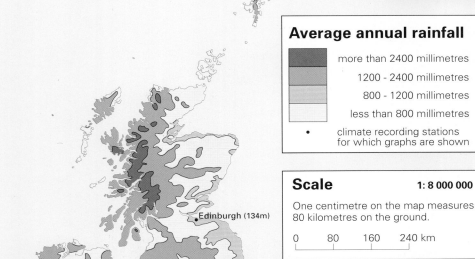

Edinburgh (134m)

•Belfast (17m)

Cambridge (12m)

Cardiff (61m)

Scale   1: 16 000 000

One centimetre on the map represents 160 kilometres on the ground.

0   160   320   480 km

The water cycle

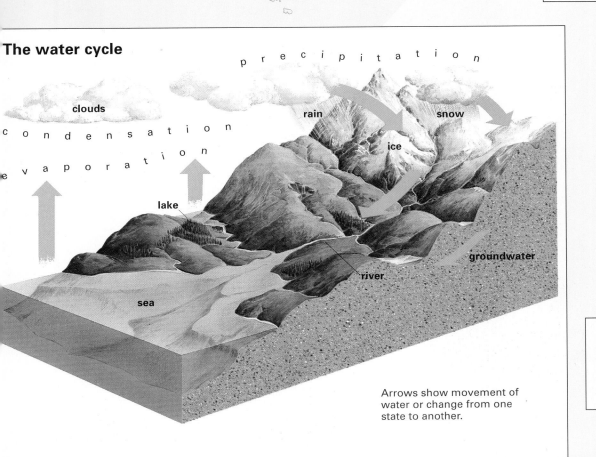

p r e c i p i t a t i o n

clouds

c o n d e n s a t i o n

e v a p o r a t i o n

rain

snow

ice

lake

river

groundwater

sea

Arrows show movement of water or change from one state to another.

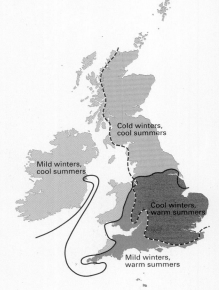

Cold winters, cool summers

Mild winters, cool summers

Cool winters, warm summers

Mild winters, warm summers

Climate regions

- - - - - average January temperature (4°C)
- ——— average July temperature (16°C)

Transverse Mercator Projection
© Oxford University Press

Population structure of the United Kingdom

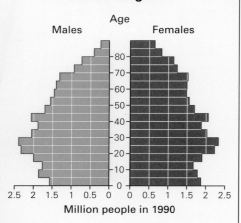

Males   Age   Females

2.5 2 1.5 1 0.5 0   0 0.5 1 1.5 2 2.5

Million people in 1990

Population density

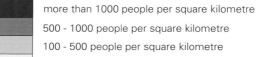

- more than 1000 people per square kilometre
- 500 - 1000 people per square kilometre
- 100 - 500 people per square kilometre
- less than 100 person per square kilometre

- – – – international boundary
- ——— national boundary
- ——— county, region, or district boundary

Major cities

- ● with more than 6 million people
- ● with 1 million people
- ● with between 500 000 and 1 million people
- • with between 100 000 and 500 000 people

Scale

1: 8 000 000

One centimetre on the map represents 80 kilometres on the ground.

0   80   160   240 km

British Isles population data

United Kingdom	Overall population density 241 people per square kilometre
Republic of Ireland	Overall population density 52 people per square kilometre

Total population 1995

England	48.7 million people
Wales	2.9 million people
Scotland	5.1 million people
Northern Ireland	1.6 million people
United Kingdom	58.4 million people
Republic of Ireland	3.6 million people

Population change

Change in population in each county, region or district, 1981 - 1991

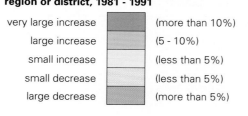

very large increase	(more than 10%)
large increase	(5 - 10%)
small increase	(less than 5%)
small decrease	(less than 5%)
large decrease	(more than 5%)

- – – – international boundary
- ——— national boundary
- ——— county, region, or district boundary

Farming, forestry and fishing

▨	mostly livestock farms (cattle are kept for meat)
▨	mostly hill farms (sheep are kept for meat and wool)
▨	mostly dairy farms (cows are kept for milk)
▨	mostly arable farms (crops are grown)

Many farms in Britain are mixed farms. Farmers grow crops and keep animals.

🌲	forestry (trees are planted for wood)
✳	market gardening (fruit and vegetables are grown)
▨	no farming (built-up areas)
⛵	fishing port
▨	main fishing grounds
----	international boundary

Scale

1: 8 000 000

One centimetre on the map represents 80 kilometres on the ground.

0   80   160   240 km

United Kingdom employment structure

The number of people employed in each activity , 1995

Primary activity
agriculture, farming, fishing, mining, and quarrying

Secondary activity
manufacturing industry

Tertiary activity
energy and water supply, construction, transport and other services

Quaternary activity
information services

0 1 2 3 4 5 6 7 8 9 10 11 12 13
million people

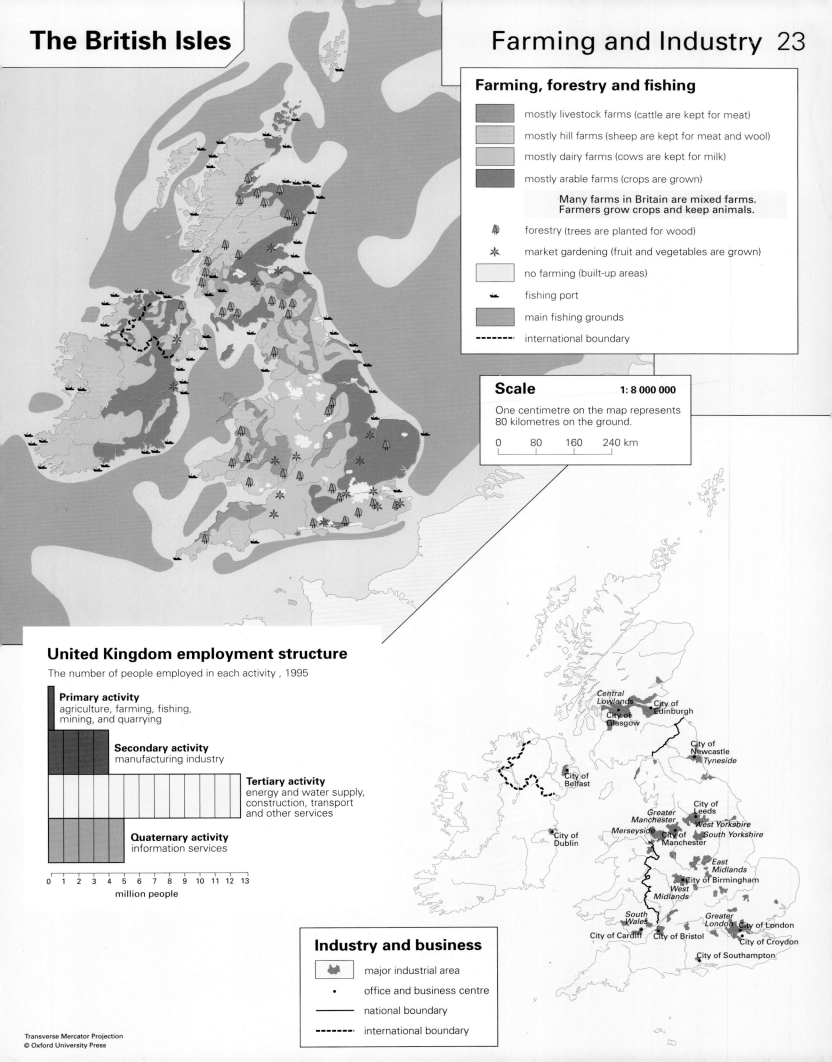

Central Lowlands
City of Edinburgh
City of Glasgow
City of Newcastle
Tyneside
City of Belfast
City of Leeds
Greater Manchester
West Yorkshire
Merseyside
City of Manchester
South Yorkshire
City of Dublin
East Midlands
City of Birmingham
West Midlands
South Wales
Greater London
City of London
City of Cardiff
City of Bristol
City of Croydon
City of Southampton

Industry and business

▨	major industrial area
•	office and business centre
——	national boundary
----	international boundary

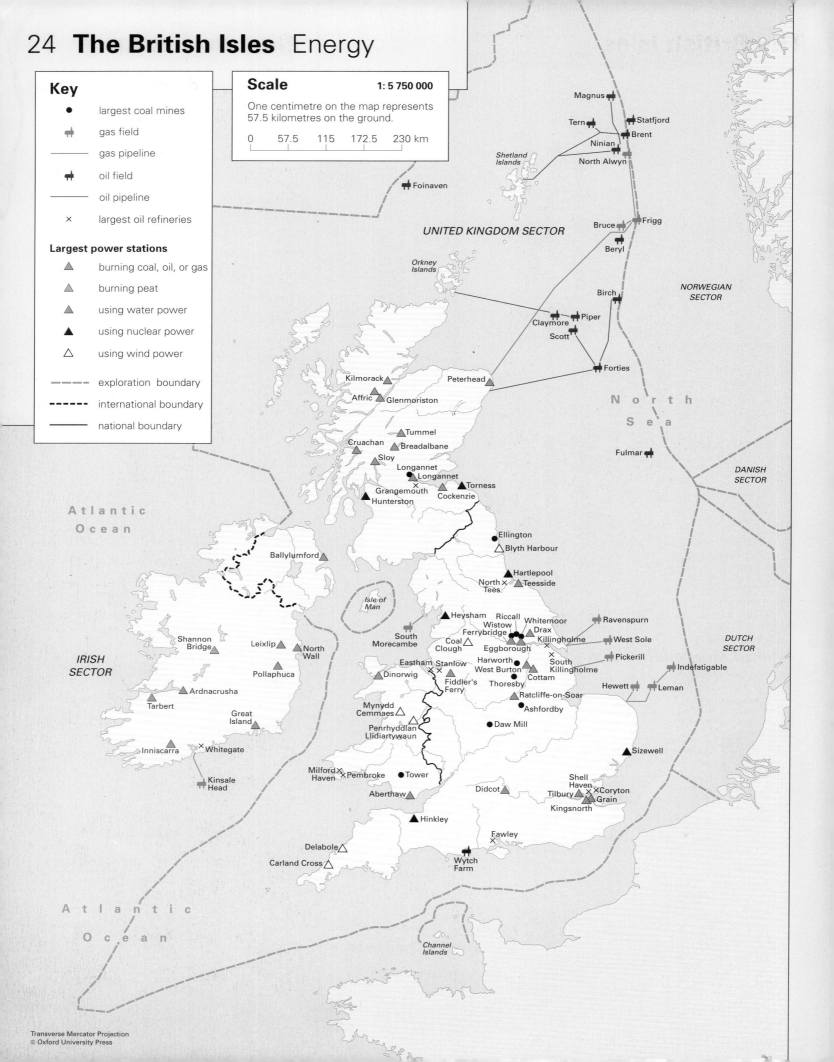

Key

- ● largest coal mines
- ⛟ gas field
- —— gas pipeline
- ⛾ oil field
- —— oil pipeline
- × largest oil refineries

Largest power stations

- ▲ burning coal, oil, or gas
- ▲ burning peat
- ▲ using water power
- ▲ using nuclear power
- △ using wind power

- –––– exploration boundary
- ‐‐‐‐ international boundary
- —— national boundary

Scale   1: 5 750 000

One centimetre on the map represents 57.5 kilometres on the ground.

0   57.5   115   172.5   230 km

Magnus
Tern
Statfjord
Brent
Ninian
North Alwyn
Shetland Islands

Foinaven

UNITED KINGDOM SECTOR

Bruce
Frigg
Beryl

Orkney Islands

NORWEGIAN SECTOR

Birch
Claymore   Piper
Scott

Forties

N o r t h
S e a

Kilmorack
Affric
Glenmoriston
Peterhead

Fulmar

DANISH SECTOR

Tummel
Cruachan
Breadalbane
Sloy
Longannet
Longannet
Grangemouth
Hunterston
Cockenzie
Torness

A t l a n t i c
O c e a n

Ellington
Blyth Harbour

Ballylumford

Hartlepool
North Tees   Teesside

Isle of Man

Heysham
Riccall   Whitemoor
Wistow   Drax
Ferrybridge
Ravenspurn
Coal Clough
Eggborough   Killingholme
West Sole
South Morecambe
Pickerill
Eastham   Stanlow
Harworth   South Killingholme
West Burton   Indefatigable
Fiddler's Ferry   Cottam
Thoresby
Hewett   Leman

Shannon Bridge
Leixlip
North Wall
Pollaphuca

IRISH SECTOR

Dinorwig

DUTCH SECTOR

Ardnacrusha
Tarbert

Mynydd Cemmaes
Ratcliffe-on-Soar
Ashfordby
Daw Mill

Sizewell

Great Island
Inniscarra   Whitegate
Kinsale Head

Penrhyddlan Llidiartywaun

Milford Haven   Pembroke
Tower

Shell Haven
Tilbury   Coryton
Grain
Kingsnorth

Aberthaw
Didcot

Hinkley

Fawley

Delabole
Carland Cross
Wytch Farm

A t l a n t i c
O c e a n

Channel Islands

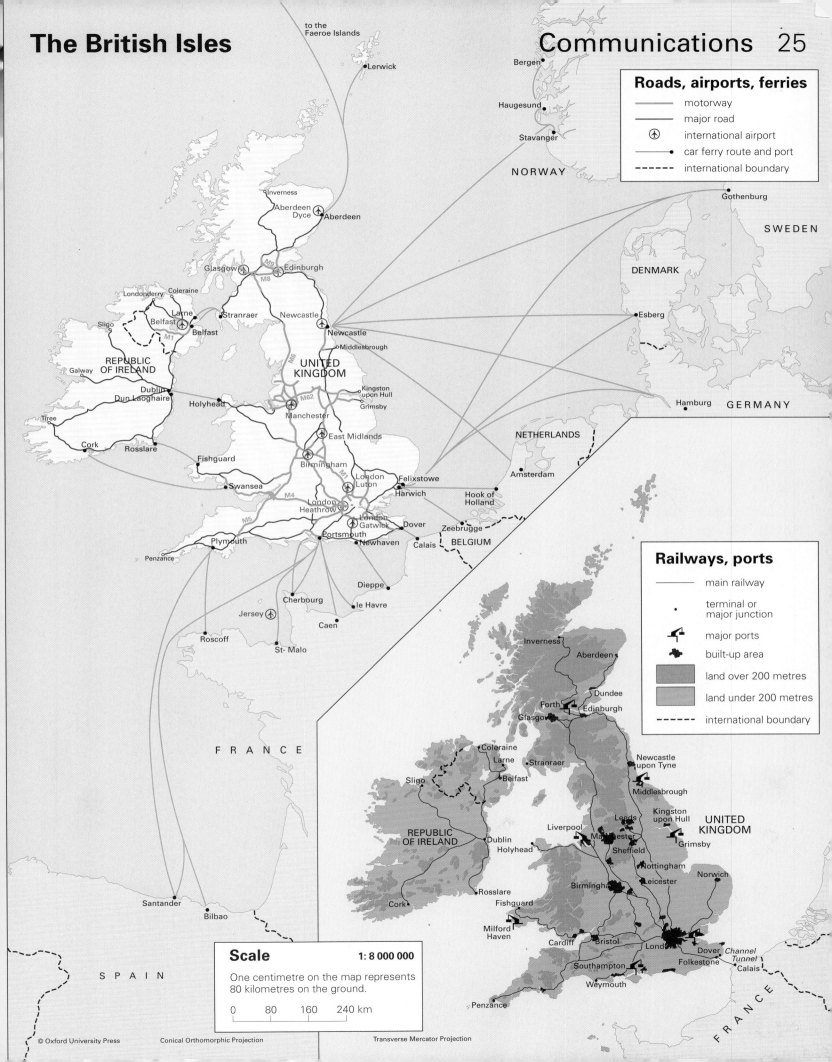

Roads, airports, ferries
— motorway
— major road
⊕ international airport
— car ferry route and port
----- international boundary

Railways, ports
— main railway
· terminal or major junction
⚓ major ports
■ built-up area
land over 200 metres
land under 200 metres
----- international boundary

to the Faeroe Islands
Lerwick

Bergen
Haugesund
Stavanger
NORWAY

Gothenburg
SWEDEN

DENMARK

Esberg

Hamburg
GERMANY

NETHERLANDS
Amsterdam
Hook of Holland
Zeebrugge
BELGIUM
Calais

Inverness
Aberdeen Dyce · Aberdeen
Glasgow · Edinburgh
M8 M9
Londonderry · Coleraine
Sligo · Belfast · Stranraer · Newcastle
Larne · Belfast · Newcastle · Middlesbrough
M1
Galway
REPUBLIC OF IRELAND
UNITED KINGDOM
M6
Dublin · Kingston upon Hull
Dun Laoghaire · Holyhead · Grimsby
M62
Manchester
Tiree
East Midlands
Cork
Rosslare
Birmingham
M1
Fishguard
London Luton · Felixstowe
Swansea · Harwich
M4
London Heathrow
M5
London Gatwick · Dover
Plymouth · Portsmouth · Newhaven
Penzance · Dieppe
Cherbourg · le Havre
Jersey
Caen
Roscoff
St-Malo

FRANCE

Santander
Bilbao

SPAIN

Scale 1: 8 000 000
One centimetre on the map represents 80 kilometres on the ground.
0   80   160   240 km

Inverness
Aberdeen
Dundee
Forth · Edinburgh
Glasgow
Coleraine
Larne · Stranraer
Belfast
Newcastle upon Tyne
Middlesbrough
Sligo
Kingston upon Hull
UNITED KINGDOM
Liverpool · Leeds
REPUBLIC OF IRELAND
Dublin · Manchester · Grimsby
Holyhead · Sheffield
Nottingham
Birmingham · Leicester · Norwich
Rosslare
Fishguard
Milford Haven
Cardiff · Bristol · London
Dover
Channel Tunnel
Folkestone · Calais
Southampton
Weymouth
Penzance
Cork

FRANCE

© Oxford University Press   Conical Orthomorphic Projection   Transverse Mercator Projection

Key

- built-up areas
- most polluted rivers and estuaries
- most polluted beaches and coastline
- ▼ sea dumping sites for sewage waste
- ▽ sea dumping sites for industrial waste
- ✱✲ accidental oil spills, 1995

Areas worst affected by acid rain

- very heavy pollution
- heavy pollution
- moderate pollution
- light pollution
- very light pollution
- --- international boundary
- ⋯ national boundary

Scale

1: 4 500 000

One centimetre on the map represents 45 kilometres on the ground.

0   45   90   135   180 km

Sulphur emissions

Industrial sites in the United Kingdom emitting the largest amounts of sulphur, in 1990–92.

thousand tonnes of sulphur

- ⬤ over 100
- ● 50–100
- • 30–50

Source: The Swedish NGO Secretariat on Acid Rain

Scale 1: 12 000 000

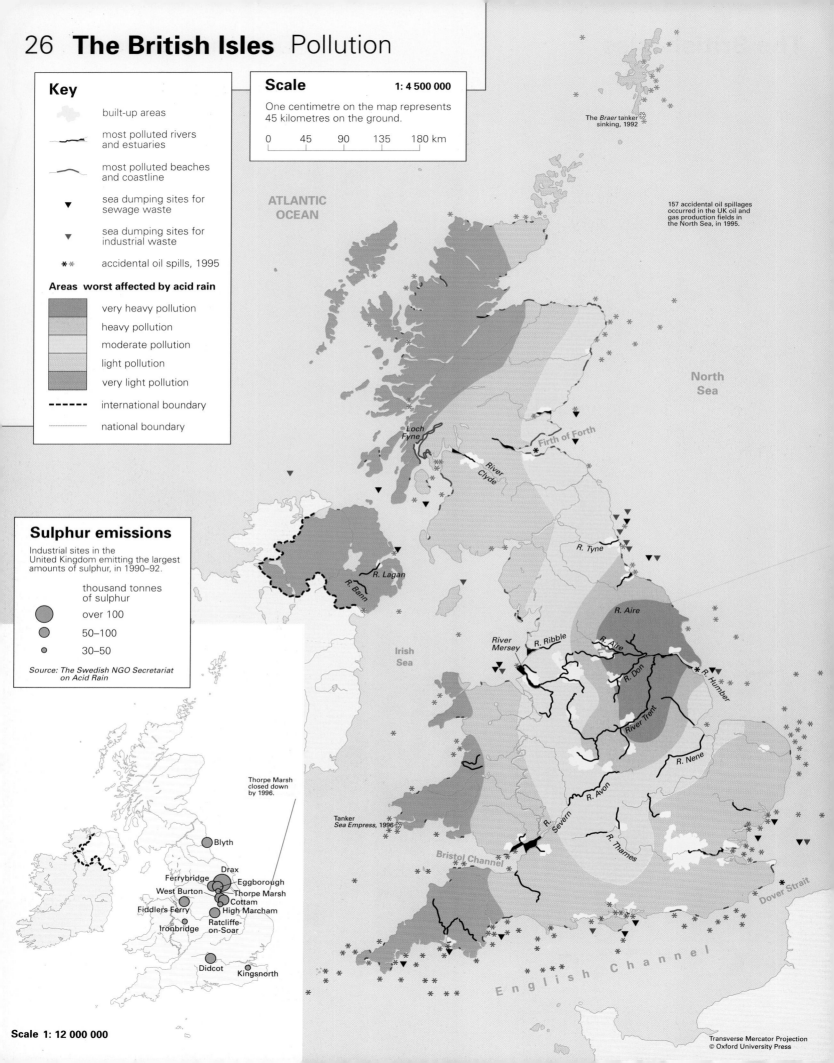

ATLANTIC OCEAN

The *Braer* tanker sinking, 1992

157 accidental oil spillages occurred in the UK oil and gas production fields in the North Sea, in 1995.

North Sea

Loch Fyne

Firth of Forth

River Clyde

R. Tyne

R. Lagan

R. Bann

R. Aire

River Mersey

R. Ribble

R. Aire

R. Don

R. Humber

Irish Sea

River Trent

R. Nene

R. Avon

R. Severn

R. Thames

Tanker *Sea Empress*, 1996

Bristol Channel

Dover Strait

English Channel

Thorpe Marsh closed down by 1996.

Blyth

Drax

Ferrybridge

Eggborough

West Burton

Thorpe Marsh

Cottam

Fiddlers Ferry

High Marcham

Ironbridge

Ratcliffe-on-Soar

Didcot

Kingsnorth

Transverse Mercator Projection
© Oxford University Press

National Parks

National Park

land over 200 metres

land under 200 metres

major built-up area

national boundary

international boundary

World Heritage Sites

Sites and monuments of world-wide natural (★) and cultural heritage (★), considered to be of such exceptional interest and value that their protection is agreed by international cooperation.

Aberdeen

Dundee

Glasgow

Edinburgh

Glenveagh

Northumberland

Newcastle upon Tyne

Belfast

Middlesbrough

Connemara

Lake District

North York Moors

Yorkshire Dales

Dublin

Leeds

Kingston upon Hull

Manchester

Liverpool

Sheffield

Peak District

Killarney

Snowdonia

Nottingham

Leicester

Birmingham

Norwich

Pembrokeshire Coast

Brecon Beacons

Cardiff

Bristol

London

Exmoor

Southampton

Dartmoor

St Kilda ★

Giant's Causeway ★

★ Hadrian's Wall
★ Durham Castle/ Cathedral

★ Fountain's Abbey/ Studley Royal Park

Castles/Town Walls of King Edward ★

Ironbridge Gorge ★

★ Blenheim Palace

★ Westminster Palace/Abbey

Bath ★

★ Stonehenge/ Avebury

Scale

1: 8 000 000

One centimetre on the map represents 80 kilometres on the ground.

0   80   160   240 km

Other protected areas

Areas of Outstanding Natural Beauty (England, Wales, Northern Ireland); National Scenic Areas (Scotland)

Heritage Coast (England and Wales); Coastal Conservation Zones (Scotland); Conservation designated coast (Northern Ireland);

major built-up area

national boundary

international boundary

South Lewis, Harris and North Uist

Wester Ross

Cairngorm Mountains

Ben Nevis and Glen Coe

Jura

Loch Lomond

Upper Tweeddale

Antrim Coast and Glens

Sperrin

North Pennines

Mourne

Nidderdale

Forest of Bowland

Anglesey

Clwydian Range

Lincolnshire Wolds

LLeyn

Norfolk Coast

Shropshire Hills

The Broads Authority

Wye Valley

Cotswolds

Suffolk Coast and Heaths

Gower

North Wessex Downs

Chilterns

Cranbourne Chase

Surrey Hills

High Weald

Kent Downs

Blackdown Hills

New Forest

Sussex Downs

Bodmin Moor

Dorset

Isle of Wight

Key

- - - - -	international boundary
———	national boundary
———	motorway and main road
———	railway
⊕	main airport
~~	river
	lake
▲	peak or highest point

towns

	built-up areas
■	largest towns
●	large towns
•	other towns

Land height

measured in metres above sea level

	more than 1000 m
	500 - 1000 m
	200 - 500 m
	100 - 200 m
	less than 100 m
	land below sea level

Scale

1 : 4 500 000

One centimetre on the map represents 45 kilometres on the ground.

0   45   90   135   180 km

© Oxford University Press
Transverse Mercator Projection

Shetland Islands

Orkney Islands

Cape Wrath

Outer Hebrides

Lewis

Skye

NORTHWEST HIGHLANDS

Inverness

Loch Ness

Great Glen

River Spey

CAIRNGORMS

River Dee

Aberdeen

1344m ▲ Ben Nevis

GRAMPIAN MOUNTAINS

R. Tay

SCOTLAND

Dundee

Mull

Loch Lomond

Firth of Forth

Glasgow

Edinburgh

River Clyde

UNITED KINGDOM

NORTHERN IRELAND

Islay

Ayr

SOUTHERN UPLANDS

R. Tweed

CHEVIOT HILLS

Coleraine

Londonderry

R. Bann

ANTRIM MOUNTAINS

Larne

Stranraer

Carlisle

Newcastle upon Tyne

River Tyne

Sunderland

NORTH Sea

Sligo

Lough Neagh

River Erne

Belfast

Isle of Man

LAKE DISTRICT

978m ▲ Scafell Pike

River Eden

River Tees

Middlesbrough

NORTH YORK MOORS

NORTH ATLANTIC OCEAN

REPUBLIC OF IRELAND

Lough Corrib

R. Boyne

852m ▲ Slieve Donard

Irish Sea

PENNINES

River Ouse

Bradford

Leeds

Kingston-upon-Hull

Galway

River Shannon

R. Liffey

Dublin

WICKLOW MOUNTAINS

Anglesey

Holyhead

Manchester

Liverpool

River Mersey

River Aire

Sheffield

River Humber

ENGLAND

Tiree

River Blackwater

River Suir

Barrow

River

1085m ▲ Snowdon

R. Dee

Nottingham

THE WASH

R. Wensum

1041m ▲ Carrauntoohill

Cork

Rosslare

WALES

CAMBRIAN MOUNTAINS

River Severn

R. Trent

Leicester

THE FENS

Norwich

Fishguard

River Teifi

Cardigan Bay

R. Wye

River Avon

Wolverhampton

Birmingham

Northampton

R. Great Ouse

R. Stour

Swansea

River Tywi

River Usk

BRECON BEACONS

Newport

Cardiff

COTSWOLD HILLS

Oxford

CHILTERN HILLS

Luton

Southend-on-Sea

Margate

Bristol Channel

Bristol

SALISBURY PLAIN

Reading

R. Thames

London

NORTH DOWNS

Dover

EXMOOR

R. Exe

Southampton

Bournemouth

SOUTH DOWNS

Portsmouth

Brighton

Strait of Dover

Calais

DARTMOOR

Exeter

Weymouth

Isle of Wight

Boulogne-sur-Mer

Land's End

Penzance

Plymouth

Isles of Scilly

English Channel

FRANCE

Cherbourg

le Havre

Rouen

R. Seine

Channel Islands

58°N

60°N

56°N

54°N

52°N

50°N

Prime Meridian

Key

- – – – county or region boundary
- ——— motorway and main road
- ——— railway
- ⊕ main airport
- ∿∿ river
- lake
- ▲ peak or highest point

towns
- • other towns

Land height

measured in metres above sea level

- 200 - 500 m
- 100 - 200 m
- less than 100 m

Scale

1: 1 000 000

One centimetre on the map represents 10 kilometres on the ground.

0 10 20 30 40 50 km

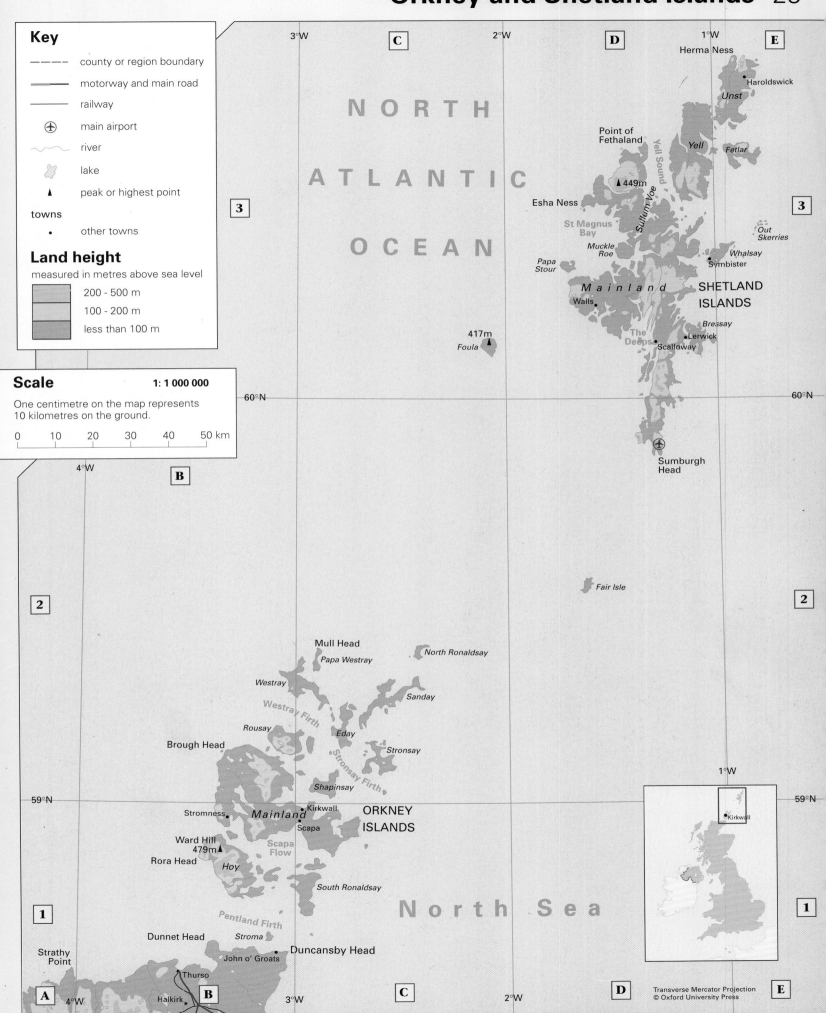

NORTH

ATLANTIC

OCEAN

3°W C 2°W D 1°W E

Herma Ness

Haroldswick

Unst

Point of Fethaland

Yell Sound

Yell

Fetlar

▲449m

Esha Ness

3

St Magnus Bay

Out Skerries

Muckle Roe

Whalsay

Papa Stour

Symbister

Mainland

SHETLAND ISLANDS

Walls

Bressay

The Deeps

Lerwick

417m

Scalloway

Foula ▲

60°N   60°N

⊕
Sumburgh Head

Fair Isle

2   2

Mull Head

Papa Westray

North Ronaldsay

Westray

Westray Firth

Sanday

Rousay

Eday

Brough Head

Stronsay

Stronsay Firth

Shapinsay

1°W

59°N   Stromness •Kirkwall ORKNEY   59°N
              Mainland   ISLANDS
                         Scapa
Ward Hill   •Kirkwall
479m ▲   Scapa
Rora Head   Flow
             Hoy

             South Ronaldsay

                                    North Sea

1   1

Pentland Firth

Dunnet Head   Stroma

Strathy Point   Duncansby Head

                 John o' Groats

A 4°W • Thurso B 3°W C 2°W D E

Halkirk

Transverse Mercator Projection
© Oxford University Press

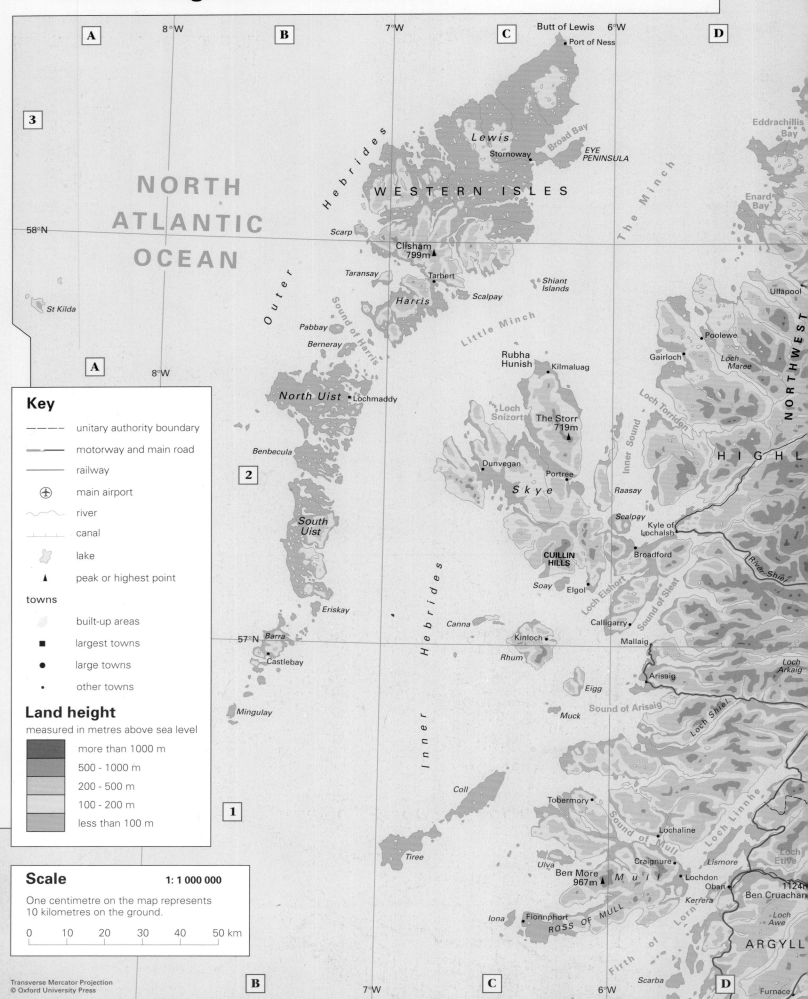

Key

- – – – – unitary authority boundary
- ━━━━ motorway and main road
- ─── railway
- ✈ main airport
- 〜 river
- ┼┼┼┼ canal
- lake
- ▲ peak or highest point

towns

- built-up areas
- ■ largest towns
- ● large towns
- • other towns

Land height

measured in metres above sea level

- more than 1000 m
- 500 - 1000 m
- 200 - 500 m
- 100 - 200 m
- less than 100 m

Scale   1: 1 000 000

One centimetre on the map represents
10 kilometres on the ground.

0   10   20   30   40   50 km

Transverse Mercator Projection
© Oxford University Press

5°W
Cape Wrath
E
4°W
Strathy Point
F
Dunnet Head
Stroma
John o' Groats
3°W

HIGHLANDS

Loch Eriboll
Ben Hope 927m ▲
Thurso
Halkirk
Wick

961m ▲ Ben Klibreck
Loch nan Clar
Kinbrace
River Thurso
Morven ▲ 705m
Lybster

▲847m Canisp
▲ 998m Ben More Assynt
Loch Shin
River Helmsdale
Helmsdale

North Sea

G

3

2°W
58°N
H

Beinn Dearg 1081m
Lairg
Brora

Bonar Bridge
Dornoch
Tarbat Ness

▲1109m Sgurr Mór
▲1046m Ben Wyvis
Tain
Dornoch Firth

Cromarty Firth
Invergordon
Cromarty
Moray Firth
Branderburgh
Lossiemouth
Burghead
Portknockie
Buckie
Cullen
Portsoy
Banff
Macduff
Rosehearty
Fraserburgh

2

River Meig
Dingwall
Nairn
Forres
Elgin
R. Spey
Fochabers
Aberchirder
Turriff
Peterhead
Buchan Ness

Inverness
R. Beauly
River Nairn
Keith
River Deveron
Huntly
Ellon

Loch Mullardoch
Carn Eige 1183m
Drumnadrochit
Loch Ness
River Nairn
River Spey
Rothes
Charlestown of Aberlour
Dufftown
MORAY
Oldmeldrum
Inverurie

ND

Invermoriston
Aviemore
Grantown-on-Spey
River Don
River Don
Dyce
ABERDEEN CITY
Aberdeen

Fort Augustus
MONADHLIATH MOUNTAINS
ABERDEENSHIRE

Invergarry
Kingussie
Newtonmore
CAIRNGORMS
1244m Cairn Gorm
Aboyne
Banchory
River Dee

57°N

Loch Lochy
Ben Alder 1148m
GRAMPIAN MOUNTAINS
Braemar
▲1155m Lochnagar
Ballater
Stonehaven

ort William
▲1344m Ben Nevis
Loch Ericht
PERTHSHIRE
River North Esk
ANGUS
Laurencekirk
Inverbervie

Blackwater Reservoir
AND
KINROSS
Pitlochry
River Isla
Milton Ness

Loch Rannoch
River Tay
Aberfeldy
Blairgowrie
Rattray
Kirriemuir
Brechin
River South Esk
Montrose

Ben Lawers 1214m
Loch Tay
Coupar Angus
Alyth
Forfar
Arbroath

Tyndrum
SCOTLAND
SIDLAW HILLS
DUNDEE CITY
Carnoustie

1

Dalmally
Crianlarich
Ben More 1174m
Loch Earn
River Earn
Crieff
Perth
Dundee
Firth of Tay

AND BUTE
Inveraray
Tarbet
Loch Katrine
Callander
Dunblane
Auchterarder
Newburgh
Cupar
St Andrews
Crail

Loch Lomond
Ben Lomond 974m
STIRLING
E
River Forth
OCHIL HILLS
4°W
F
CLACKMANNANSHIRE
Kinross
Loch Leven
Glenrothes
FIFE
Buckhaven
3°W
G
Anstruther
2°W
H

© Oxford University Press

Key

- ▬·▬·▬ international boundary
- ▬ ▬ ▬ national boundary
- ▬·▬·▬ county, district or unitary authority boundary
- ▬▬▬ motorway and main road
- ▬▬▬ railway
- ⊕ main airport
- river
- canal
- lake
- ▲ peak or highest point

towns

- built-up areas
- ■ largest towns
- ● large towns
- · other towns

Land height
measured in metres above sea level

- more than 1000 m
- 500 - 1000 m
- 200 - 500 m
- 100 - 200 m
- less than 100 m

Transverse Mercator Projection
© Oxford University Press

Edinburgh
Belfast

Scale 1: 1 000 000

One centimetre on the map represents
10 kilometres on the ground.

0 10 20 30 40 50 km

© Oxford University Press

3°W
2°W

A
4°W
B
C
D

Lockerbie

Blyt

NORTHUMBERLAND
Cramlington

55°N
Annan
R. Irthing
Haltwhistle
Newcastle upon
Tyne

Newton Stewart
Castle
Douglas
Dalbeattie
Kirkbean
River Irthing
Brampton
Hexham
R. Tyne
Gateshead

Glenluce
Gatehouse
of Fleet
Carlisle
Washington

Wigtown
Kirkcudbright
Wigton
River Eden
R. Derwent
Consett
Chester-
le-Street

Luce
Bay
Whithorn
Maryport
R. Derwent
Cross Fell
893m
River Wear
Durham

Wigtown
Bay
Cockermouth
Penrith
DURHAM
Spennymoor
Bishop

Mull of
Galloway
Workington
931m
Skiddaw
CUMBRIA
Mickle Fell
790m
Appleby-in-
Westmorland
River Tees
Auckland
Newton
Aycliffe

Keswick
Derwent
Water
Ullswater
Brough
Barnard
Castle
Darlington

3
Whitehaven
Helvellyn
950m
LAKE
Kirkby
Stephen
Richmond

St Bees Head
DISTRICT
River Swale

978m
Scafell Pike
Ambleside
River Ure
Leyburn

Point of Ayre
Seascale
Windermere
Windermere
NORTH YORKSHIRE

Ramsey
Coniston
Water
Kenda
River Lune
Whernside
737m
River Wharfe

Kirk
Michael
Snaefell
620m
R. Greta
Pen-y-Ghent
693m
Great Whernside
704m

Peel
ISLE OF
MAN
723m
Ingleborough
Ripon

South
Barrule
483m
Douglas
Dalton-in-
Furness
Morecambe
Bay
Carnforth

Castletown
Barrow-in-
Furness
Morecambe
Lancaster
River
Nidd

54°N
Heysham
560m
Ward's Stone
Skipton
Harrogate

Fleetwood
FOREST
OF
BOWLAND
River Aire

Irish Sea
River Wyre
Barnoldswick
Ilkley
Keighley

Clitheroe
Colne

Blackpool
LANCASHIRE
River Ribble
Nelson
Bradford
Leeds

Preston
Burnley
Halifax
WEST

Lytham
St Anne's
Blackburn
Brighouse
Dewsbury

Leyland
Huddersfield
YORKSHIRE

Southport
Chorley
Bury
Rochdale

2
Formby
Skelmersdale
Wigan
GREATER
MANCHESTER
Bolton
Oldham

Carmel
Head
Amlwch
Kirkby
Salford
Manchester

Holyhead
Bootle
Wallasey
MERSEYSIDE
St Helens
Sale
Stockport
The Peak
636m

Holy
Island
Birkenhead
Liverpool
Widnes
Warrington
Cheadle

ANGLESEY
Llandudno
Rhyl
River Dee
Runcorn
Macclesfield
Buxton

Bangor
Conwy
Colwyn
Bay
Ellesmere
Port
Northwich
DERBYSHIRE

Caernarfon
Bethesda
Denbigh
FLINTSHIRE
Flint
Chester
CHESHIRE
River Dove

Caernarfon
Bay
Snowdon
1085m
ABERCONWY
Mold
Winsford
Bakewell

AND
River Clwyd
Matlock

COLWYN
DENBIGHSHIRE
Crewe
Kidsgrove

53°N
Blaenau
Ffestiniog
River Dee
Wrexham
Newcastle-
under-Lyme
Stoke-on-Trent

Portmadog
WREXHAM
Ashbourne

Pwllheli
Harlech
Llangollen
Whitchurch
ENGLAND

1
Bala
Lake
Vyrnwy
Oswestry
Market
Drayton
Uttoxeter
Burton upon
Trent

Barmouth
Dolgellau
POWYS
R. Vyrnwy
Stafford
Rugeley

Cader Idris
892m
Welshpool
Newport
STAFFORDSHIRE
Lichfield

Cardigan
Bay
Machynlleth
WALES
Shrewsbury
SHROPSHIRE
Telford
407m
The Wrekin
Canock
Tamworth

© Oxford University Press
Wolverhampton

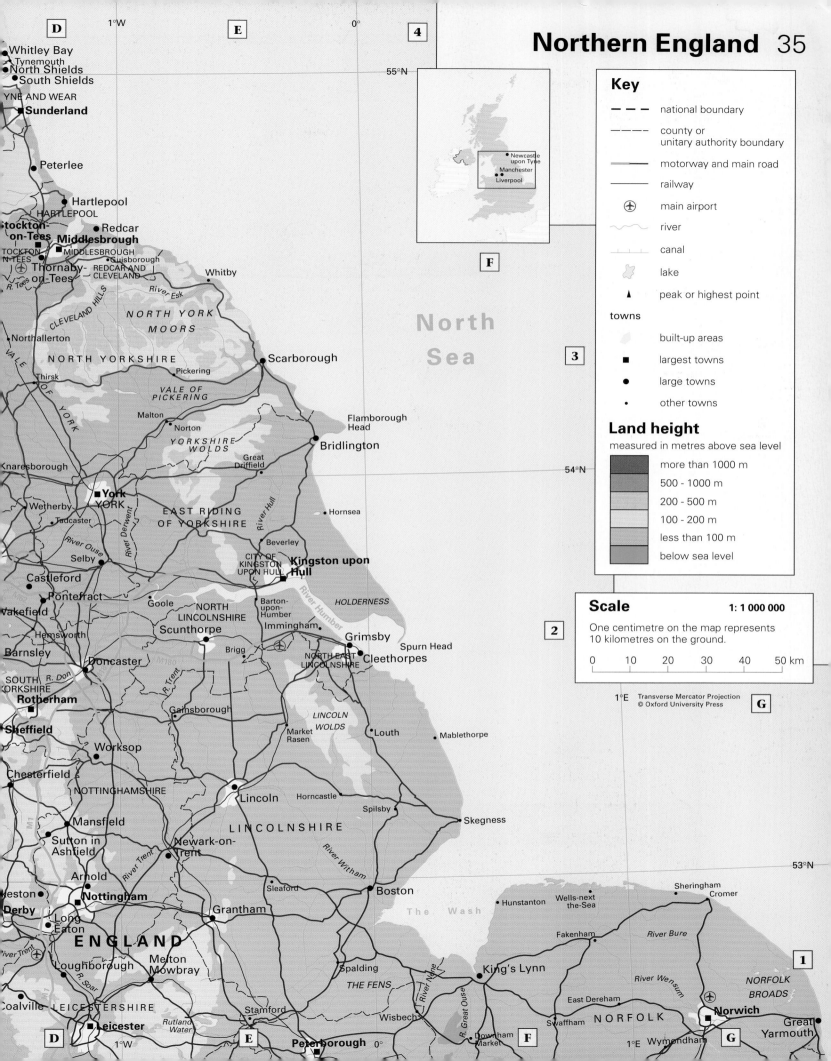

D   1°W   E   0°   4

Whitley Bay
Tynemouth
North Shields
South Shields
YNE AND WEAR
Sunderland

Peterlee

Hartlepool
HARTLEPOOL
tockton-
on-Tees   Redcar
Middlesbrough
TOCKTON-   MIDDLESBROUGH
N-TEES   Guisborough
Thornaby-   REDCAR AND
on-Tees   CLEVELAND   Whitby
R. Tees

CLEVELAND HILLS

River Esk

NORTH YORK
MOORS

Northallerton

NORTH YORKSHIRE

Thirsk   Scarborough

VALE   Pickering
OF
PICKERING

VALE OF YORK   Malton
Norton

YORKSHIRE
WOLDS

Knaresborough   Flamborough
Head

Great   Bridlington
Driffield

York   North Sea
YORK

Wetherby   River Hull
Taccaster

EAST RIDING   Hornsea
OF YORKSHIRE

River Derwent

River Ouse   Beverley

Selby   CITY OF   Kingston upon
KINGSTON   Hull
UPON HULL

Castleford

Pontefract   River Humber

Goole   HOLDERNESS
akefield   NORTH   Barton-
Hemsworth   LINCOLNSHIRE   upon-
Scunthorpe   Humber   Spurn Head
Barnsley   Immingham
R. Don   Brigg   Grimsby
Doncaster   Cleethorpes
SOUTH   NORTH EAST
ORKSHIRE   R. Trent   LINCOLNSHIRE
Rotherham

Gainsborough

Sheffield   LINCOLN
WOLDS
Worksop   Louth
Market   Mablethorpe
Chesterfield   Rasen

NOTTINGHAMSHIRE

Mansfield   Lincoln   Horncastle
Sutton in   Spilsby
Ashfield   Skegness
LINCOLNSHIRE
Arnold   Newark-on-
River Trent   Trent   River Witham

Long   Nottingham
Eaton   Grantham   53°N
Derby   Sheringham
ston   Cromer
R. Trent   Sleaford   Boston
Loughborough   Melton   Hunstanton   Wells-next-
Mowbray   the-Sea   Fakenham
R. Soar   River Bure
Spalding   King's Lynn
THE FENS   The Wash   River Wensum
Coalville LEICESTERSHIRE   River Nene   NORFOLK
Stamford   East Dereham   BROADS
Leicester   Rutland   Wisbech   NORFOLK   Norwich
Water   R. Great Ouse   Great
ENGLAND   Peterborough   0°   Downham   Swaffham   Wymondham   Yarmouth
Market   1°E   G

55°N

F

3

54°N

2

1°E   Transverse Mercator Projection
© Oxford University Press   G

1

Key

- - - national boundary

-·-·- county or
unitary authority boundary

━━━ motorway and main road

━━━ railway

⊕ main airport

〜 river

╤ canal

lake

▲ peak or highest point

towns

built-up areas

■ largest towns

● large towns

• other towns

Land height

measured in metres above sea level

more than 1000 m
500 - 1000 m
200 - 500 m
100 - 200 m
less than 100 m
below sea level

Scale   1: 1 000 000

One centimetre on the map represents
10 kilometres on the ground.

0   10   20   30   40   50 km

Formby
MERSEYSIDE
Bootle
Wallasey
Liverpool
Birkenhead

A 6°W
B
5°W
C
4°W
D
3°W

Irish Sea

Carmel Head
Amlwch
Holyhead
Holy Island
ANGLESEY
Llandudno
Rhyl
Conwy
Colwyn Bay
R. Conwy
FLINTSHIRE
Flint
Bangor
Bethesda
ABERCONWY
Denbigh
Mold
Caernarfon
AND
Snowdon 1085m
COLWYN
DENBIGHSHIRE
Wrexham
WREXHAM

3

Dublin
Dún Laoghaire
Bray
Greystones

REPUBLIC OF IRELAND

53°N
Wicklow

Arklow

Irish Sea

Caernarfon Bay

LLEYN PENINSULA
Porthmadog
Pwllheli
Harlech

Blaenau Ffestiniog
River Dee
Llangollen
Oswestry
Bala
Bala Lake
CAERNARFONSHIRE AND MERIONETHSHIRE
905m
Aran Fawddy
Lake Vyrnwy
Barmouth
Dolgellau
Cader Idris 892m
R. Vyrnwy
Welshpool

Cardigan Bay

R. Dyfi
WALES
Machynlleth
Montgomery
R. Severn

2

Cardigan Bay

752m
Plynlimon
Newtown
Llanidloes
SHROPSHIRE

Aberystwyth

CARDIGANSHIRE
Rhayader
Knighton

Aberaeron
New Quay
River Teifi
Llandrindod Wells
Kington

POWYS

Cemaes Head
Lampeter
Cardigan
River Teifi
Builth Wells

52°N
Strumble Head
Newcastle Emlyn
Llandovery
MYNYDD EPPYNT
R. Wye
Hay-on-Wye

Fishguard
MYNYDD PRESELI
R. Tywi
River Usk
Brecon
811m
BLACK MOUNTAINS

St David's Head
St David's
PEMBROKESHIRE
CARMARTHENSHIRE
Carmarthen
Llandeilo
BRECON 886m BEACONS
Abergavenny

Haverfordwest
R. Tywi
Ammanford
Merthyr Tydfil
Ebbw Vale
BLAENAU GWENT
TORFAEN
Abertillery

St Brides Bay

Milford Haven
Kidwelly
Burry Port
Pontardulais
NEATH AND PORT TALBOT
Aberdare
RHONDDA
MERTHYR TYDFIL
Pontypool
Cwmbran

1

NORTH

Pembroke
Tenby
Carmarthen Bay
SWANSEA
Neath
CYNON
TAFF
CAERPHILLY
NEWPORT

Llanelli
Rhondda
Pontypridd
Caerphilly
Newport

Swansea
GOWER
Port Talbot
BRIDGEND
CARDIFF

Worms Head

Bridgend

ATLANTIC

Cardiff

VALE OF GLAMORGAN
Barry

OCEAN

Weston-super-Mare

Bristol Channel

Bridgwater Bay

Lynton
Minehead

Ilfracombe
Dunkery Beacon 519m

Lundy
DEVON
EXMOOR

St George's Channel

Key

– – –	national boundary
–·–·–	county or unitary authority boundary
───	motorway and main road
───	railway
✈	main airport
∿	river
⊥⊥⊥	canal
🗺	lake
▲	peak or highest point

towns

	built-up areas
■	largest towns
●	large towns
•	other towns

Land height

measured in metres above sea level

	more than 1000 m
	500 - 1000 m
	200 - 500 m
	100 - 200m
	less than 100 m

Scale 1: 1 000 000

One centimetre on the map represents 10 kilometres on the ground.

0   10   20   30   40   50 km

Transverse Mercator Projection
© Oxford University Press

© Oxford University Press

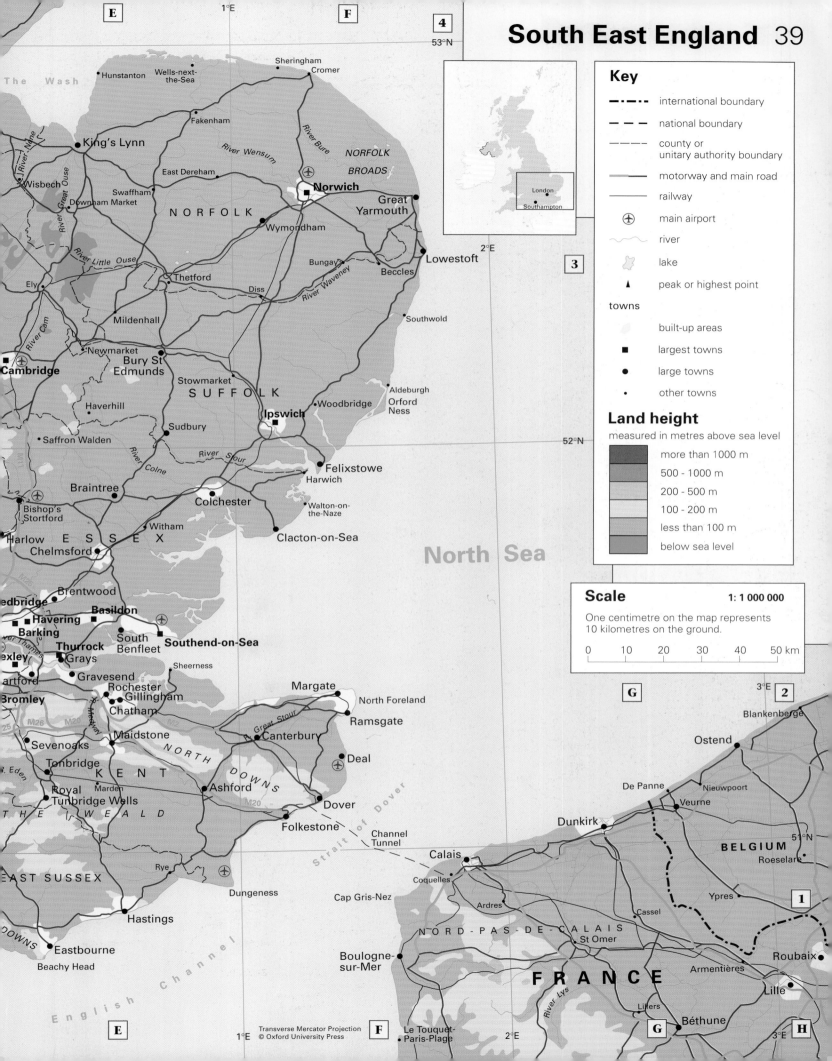

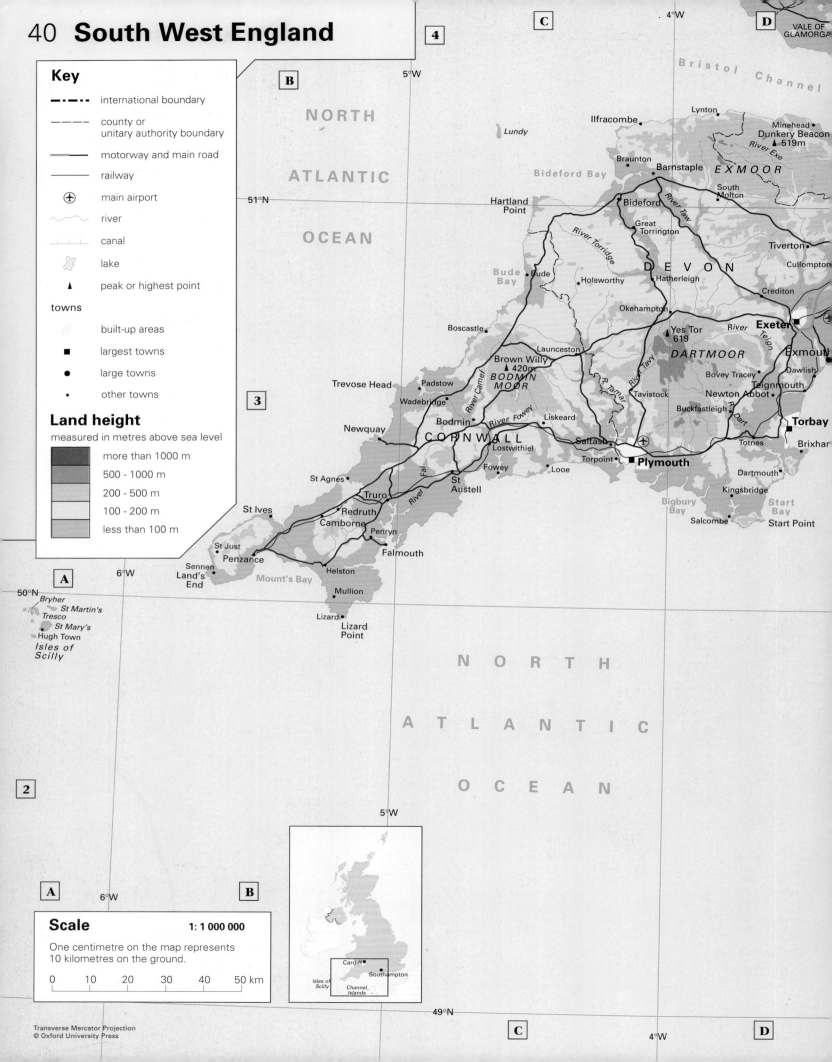

Key

- –··–··– international boundary
- – – – county or unitary authority boundary
- ——— motorway and main road
- ——— railway
- ✈ main airport
- 〰 river
- ┼┼┼ canal
- 🮑 lake
- ▲ peak or highest point

towns

- built-up areas
- ■ largest towns
- ● large towns
- • other towns

Land height

measured in metres above sea level

- more than 1000 m
- 500 – 1000 m
- 200 – 500 m
- 100 – 200 m
- less than 100 m

NORTH ATLANTIC OCEAN

Bristol Channel

VALE OF GLAMORGAN

4°W

D

5°W

B

C

NORTH ATLANTIC OCEAN

51°N

50°N

49°N

6°W

Lundy

Ilfracombe
Lynton
Minehead
Dunkery Beacon ▲ 519m
River Exe
EXMOOR
Braunton
Barnstaple
South Molton
Bideford Bay
Hartland Point
Bideford
River Taw
Great Torrington
River Torridge
Tiverton
Cullompton
DEVON
Bude Bay
Bude
Holsworthy
Hatherleigh
Crediton
Boscastle
Okehampton
Exeter
Launceston
Yes Tor ▲ 619
River Teign
Exmouth
Brown Willy ▲ 420m
BODMIN MOOR
R. Tamar
River Tavy
DARTMOOR
Dawlish
Bovey Tracey
Trevose Head
Padstow
River Camel
Tavistock
Newton Abbot
Teignmouth
Wadebridge
Buckfastleigh
River Dart
Bodmin
River Fowey
Liskeard
Newquay
CORNWALL
Lostwithiel
Saltash
Totnes
Torbay
St Agnes
Fowey
Torpoint
Brixham
Looe
Plymouth
River Fal
St Austell
Dartmouth
Truro
Redruth
Camborne
Penryn
Bigbury Bay
Kingsbridge
Start Bay
St Ives
Falmouth
Salcombe
Start Point
St Just
Penzance
Sennen
Land's End
Helston
Mount's Bay
Mullion
Lizard
Lizard Point

Bryher
St Martin's
Tresco
St Mary's
Hugh Town
Isles of Scilly

A

3

B

NORTH ATLANTIC OCEAN

5°W

2

A

6°W

B

Transverse Mercator Projection
© Oxford University Press

Scale 1: 1 000 000

One centimetre on the map represents 10 kilometres on the ground.

0 10 20 30 40 50 km

Cardiff
Southampton
Isles of Scilly
Channel Islands

C

D

D Cardiff 3°W
Clevedon
Barry
Weston-super-Mare
Bridgwater Bay
QUANTOCK HILLS
SOMERSET
Taunton
Wellington
River Tone
Honiton
Sidmouth
Seaton
Axminster
Lyme Regis
Bridport
Lyme Bay

CITY OF BRISTOL
Bristol
Kingswood
Keynsham
BATH AND NORTH EAST SOMERSET
NORTH WEST SOMERSET
Bath
MENDIP HILLS
Wells
Shepton Mallet
Glastonbury
Bridgwater
R. Parrett
River Yeo
Wincanton
Mere
Ilchester
Yeovil
Sherborne
Ilminster
Crewkerne
Chard
River Axe
River Frome
Dorchester
Weymouth
St Alban's Head
Portland Bill

3°W E M4
Chippenham
Calne
Devizes
R. Avon
Trowbridge
WILTSHIRE
Westbury SALISBURY
Warminster PLAIN
Frome
Shaftesbury
Blandford Forum
River Stour
Wimborne Minster
Wareham
Poole
Bournemouth
Christchurch
Swanage

2°W F
Andover
297m Walbury Hill
Amesbury
Stockbridge
River Test
Salisbury
Romsey
River Avon
Totton
Southampton
Ringwood
Fawley
Lymington
The Needles
ISLE OF WIGHT
Cowes
Newport
St Catherine's Point

HAMPSHIRE DOWNS
Basingstoke
M3
Winchester
HAMPSHIRE
Eastleigh
River Itchen
Alton
Petersfield
River Meon
Waterlooville
Havant
Fareham
Gosport
Portsmouth
The Solent
Ryde
Sandown
Shanklin
Selsey Bill

w Camberley G
Farnborough
Aldershot
Farnham
Haslemere
SOUTH DOWNS
WEST SUSSEX
Chichester
Bognor Regis

Woking Epsom
SURREY
Guildford
Dorking
NORTH DOWNS
Horsham
51°N
R. Arun
Littlehampton
Worthing

4

English Channel

50°N

Cap de la Hague
Auderville
Alderney
Barfleur
Cherbourg
Valognes
Guernsey
St Peter-Port
Sark
FRANCE
Baie de la Seine
2

CHANNEL
Carteret
ISLANDS
Lessay
Carentan
Isigny-sur-Mer
Bayeux
Jersey
St Helier
St-lo
River Vine
Caen
Coutainville
Coutances
River Orne
49°N
1

D 3°W E 2°W F 1°W G
© Oxford University Press

The European Union

- – – – – international boundary
- • national capital
- member country of the European Union
- countries that have applied to join the European Union

Scale
1 : 40 000 000

One centimetre on the map represents 400 kilometres on the ground.

0   400   800   1200 km

Wealth

Gross Domestic Product (GDP) per person, 1992

The annual total value of all the goods and services produced in a country divided by the number of people living in that country.

- **more than 20 000** among the top 10 countries of the world
- **15 000 – 20 000** among the top 25 countries of the world
- **10 000 – 15 000** among the top 30 countries of the world
- **5000 – 10 000** among the top 70 countries of the world
- **0 – 5000** among the top 120 countries of the world

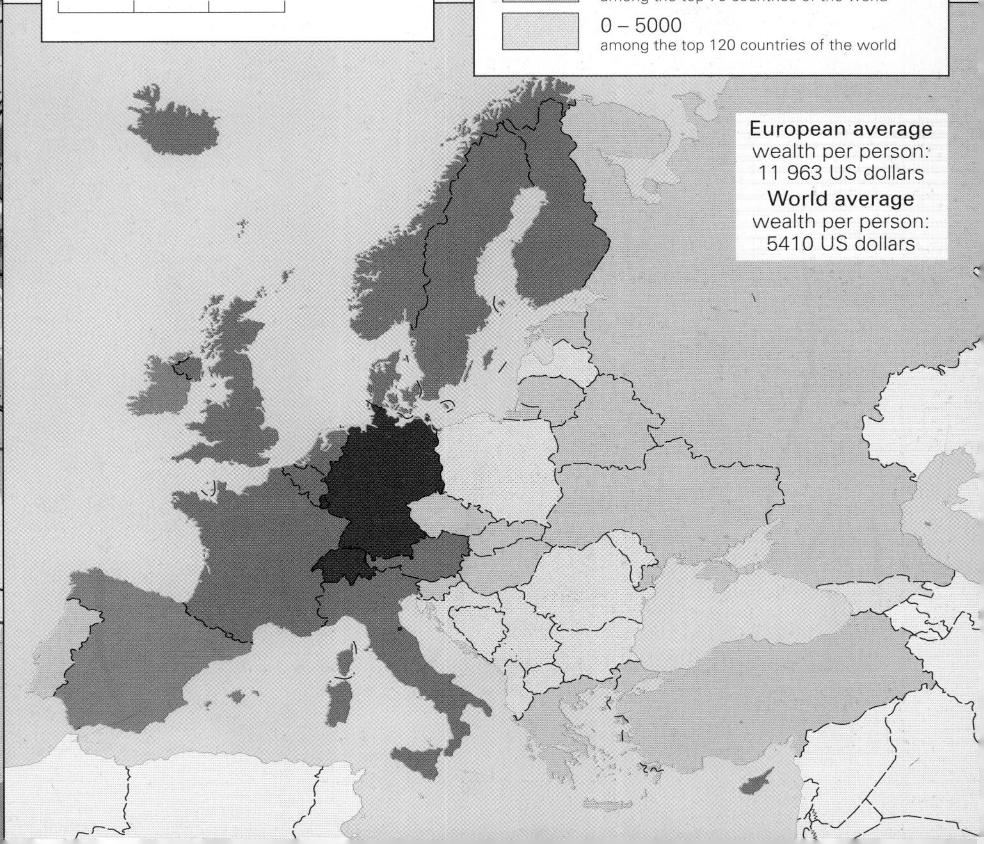

European average wealth per person: 11 963 US dollars

World average wealth per person: 5410 US dollars

Map labels (left panel)

URAL MOUNTAINS
Pechora, Ukhta, Syktyvkar, Serov, Nizhniy Tagil, Yekaterinburg (Sverdlovsk), Perm, Solikamsk, Berezniki, Kotlas, Glazov, Izhevsk, Kirov (Vyatka), Ufa, Naberezhnye Chelny, Nizhnekamsk, Sterlitamak
Severodvinsk, Arkhangelsk, North Dvina, Vologda, nerepovets, Rybinsk Reservoir, Yaroslavl, Ivanovo, Vladimir, Nizhniy-Novgorod (Gorkiy), Kazan', Cheboksary, Volga, Oka
Moscow, Ryazan, Ul'yanovsk (Simbirsk), Tol'yatti, Samara (Kuybyshev), Orenburg
RUSSIAN FEDERATION (RUSSIA)
Bryansk, Orel, Tula, Lipetsk, Kursk, Voronezh, Tambov, Penza, Saratov, Engel's, Balakovo, Ural'sk, Ural
KAZAKHSTAN
Sumy, Kharkov, Don, Donets, Luhans'k, Volgograd, Tsimlyansk Reservoir, Astrakhan
Kremenchuk, Dnipropetrovsk, Donetsk, Shakhty, Rostov-on-Don, Caspian Sea
rovohrad, Kryvyy Rih (Krivoy Rog), Zaporizhzhya, Mariupol, Stavropol
Mykolayiv (Nikolayev), Kherson, Sea of Azov, Krasnodar, Maykop, Pyatigorsk, Nalchik, Makhachkala, Grozny
Crimea, Simferopol, Sochi, Mt. Elbrus 5642 m, Vladikavkaz, CAUCASUS, Kutaisi, Gyandzha
Sevastopol, Black Sea, Sukhumi, GEORGIA, Tbilisi, Batumi, AZERBAIJAN
Samsun, Trabzon, ARMENIA, Yerevan, Mt. Ararat 5123 m, Araks
Zonguldak, Erzurum, IRAN, Lake Van, Lake Urmia
zmit, Ankara, Kirikkale, Sivas, Elâziğ, Diyarbakir
Eskişehir, TURKEY, Lake Tuz, Kayseri, Malatya, Firat, Arbil, Mosul, Kirkuk
Konya, Gaziantep, Euphrates, Tigris
Antalya, Adana, Mersin, Aleppo
Latakia, Hamah, SYRIA
Nicosia, Homs, IRAQ
CYPRUS, Limassol, Tripoli, LEBANON, Zahle, Beirut, Damascus
Haifa, Tel Aviv-Jaffa, ISRAEL, Jerusalem, Irbid, Zarqa, Amman, JORDAN, SAUDI ARABIA
Port Said, Beersheba, Jauf
Alexandria, EGYPT, Giza, Cairo, Suez, Mt. Sinai 2641 m, Tabuk, ARABIA

Map labels (right panel)

SWEDEN, FINLAND, Stockholm, Helsinki
DENMARK, Copenhagen
Dublin, REPUBLIC OF IRELAND, UNITED KINGDOM, London, NETHERLANDS, Amsterdam, Berlin, Warsaw, POLAND
Brussels, BELGIUM, GERMANY, LUXEMBOURG, Luxembourg
Paris, FRANCE, Bern, SWITZERLAND, Vienna, AUSTRIA, Budapest, HUNGARY
PORTUGAL, Madrid, SPAIN, ITALY, Rome, Ankara, TURKEY
Lisbon, GREECE, Athens
MALTA, Valletta

Climatic regions

Very dry

with no reliable rain

with a little rain

**Influenced by the sea:
warm summers, mild winters**

with dry summers
(Mediterranean type)

with no dry season

Cool

rain all year

Cold polar

no warm season
and fairly dry

Mountain

height of the land
strongly affects
the climate

Ocean currents

→ warm

→ cold

Climate recording stations

• climate recording
stations for which
graphs are shown

Scale

1: 40 000 000

One centimetre on the map represents
400 kilometres on the ground.

0   400   800   1200 km

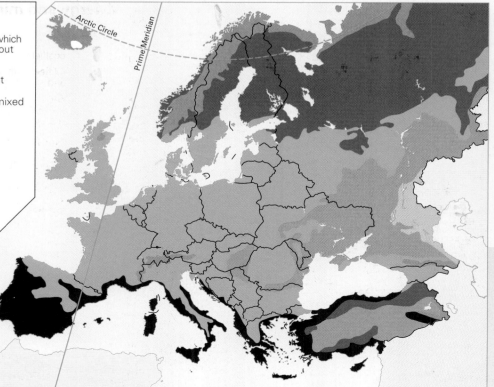

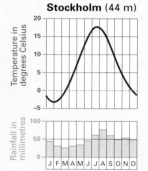

Stockholm (44 m)

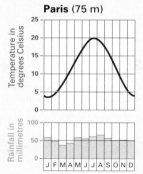

Paris (75 m)

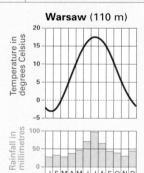

Warsaw (110 m)

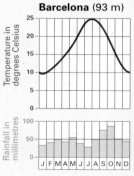

Barcelona (93 m)

Ecosystems

Vegetation types are those which
would occur naturally without
interference by people.

coniferous forest

deciduous and mixed
forest

evergreen trees
and shrubs

temperate
grasslands

semi-desert

tundra

ice

mountains

—— country
boundary

More information
about these
ecosystems can be
found on page 8.

Stockholm
Mean annual rainfall : 524 mm
Mean January temperature : -3.0°C
Mean July temperature : 18.0°C

Paris
Mean annual rainfall : 589 mm
Mean January temperature : 3.5°C
Mean July temperature : 20.0°C

Warsaw
Mean annual rainfall : 525 mm
Mean January temperature : -3.0°C
Mean July temperature : 19.5°C

Barcelona
Mean annual rainfall : 587 mm
Mean January temperature : 9.5°C
Mean July temperature : 24.5°C

Almeria
Mean annual rainfall : 233 mm
Mean January temperature : 12.0°C
Mean July temperature : 25.0°C

Conical Orthomorphic Projection

© Oxford University Press

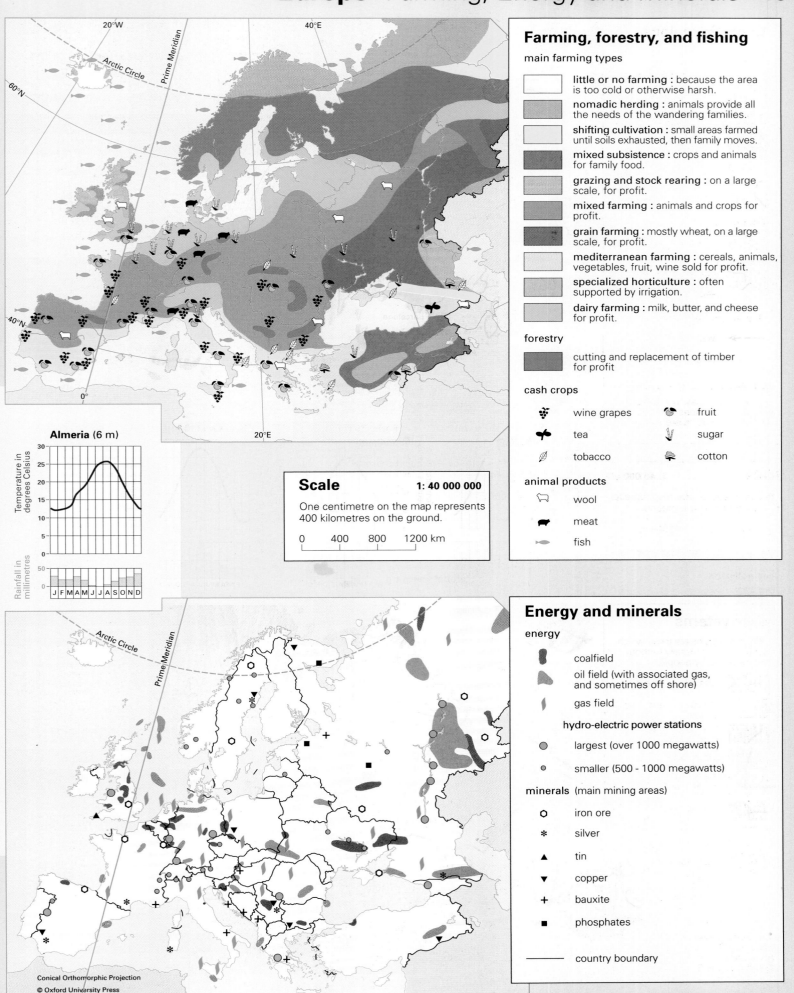

Farming, forestry, and fishing

main farming types

- **little or no farming** : because the area is too cold or otherwise harsh.
- **nomadic herding** : animals provide all the needs of the wandering families.
- **shifting cultivation** : small areas farmed until soils exhausted, then family moves.
- **mixed subsistence** : crops and animals for family food.
- **grazing and stock rearing** : on a large scale, for profit.
- **mixed farming** : animals and crops for profit.
- **grain farming** : mostly wheat, on a large scale, for profit.
- **mediterranean farming** : cereals, animals, vegetables, fruit, wine sold for profit.
- **specialized horticulture** : often supported by irrigation.
- **dairy farming** : milk, butter, and cheese for profit.

forestry

- cutting and replacement of timber for profit

cash crops

wine grapes		fruit	
tea		sugar	
tobacco		cotton	

animal products

- wool
- meat
- fish

Almeria (6 m)

Temperature in degrees Celsius

Rainfall in millimetres

J F M A M J J A S O N D

Scale   1 : 40 000 000

One centimetre on the map represents 400 kilometres on the ground.

0   400   800   1200 km

Energy and minerals

energy

- coalfield
- oil field (with associated gas, and sometimes off shore)
- gas field

hydro-electric power stations

- largest (over 1000 megawatts)
- smaller (500 - 1000 megawatts)

minerals (main mining areas)

- iron ore
- silver
- tin
- copper
- bauxite
- phosphates

— country boundary

Conical Orthomorphic Projection
© Oxford University Press

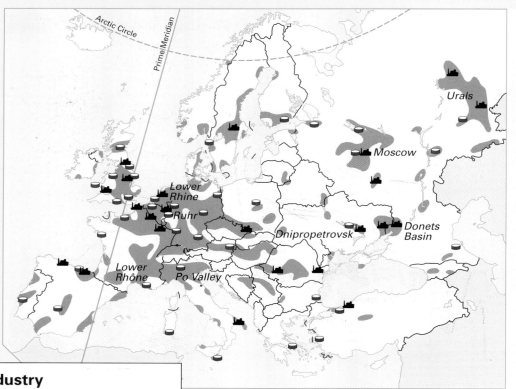

Arctic Circle
Prime Meridian
Urals
Moscow
Lower Rhine
Ruhr
Dnipropetrovsk
Donets Basin
Lower Rhône
Po Valley

Industry

industrial areas

iron and steel

oil refining and petro-chemicals

country boundary

Scale
1: 40 000 000

One centimetre on the map represents
400 kilometres on the ground.

0   400   800   1200 km

Population structure of the United Kingdom

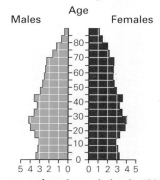

Age
Males   Females

5 4 3 2 1 0   0 1 2 3 4 5

percent of total population in 1990
Total population : 57.4 million

Population structure of France

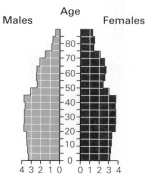

Age
Males   Females

4 3 2 1 0   0 1 2 3 4

percent of total population in 1993
Total population : 57.5 million

Environmental issues

sea pollution

areas severely polluted for all or part of the year

areas persistently affected by pollution

▼ deep sea dump sites

✳ major oil spills (over 100 000 tonnes)

✴ major oil spills (less than 100 000 tonnes)

acid rain A pH scale measures acidity. Unaffected rain water is slightly acidic with a pH of 5.6

pH less than 4.2 (the most acidic)

pH 4.2 - 4.6

pH 4.6 - 5.0

air pollution

◆ cities where sulphur dioxide emmissions are recorded, and exceed recommended levels

industrial sites emmitting the largest amounts of sulphur, in 1990-92

thousands of tonnes of sulphur

◯ over 200

◯ 100 - 200

◦ 50 - 100

∘ 30 - 50

global warming
addition of greenhouse gases in tonnes of carbon per person
(look at the world map on page 17)

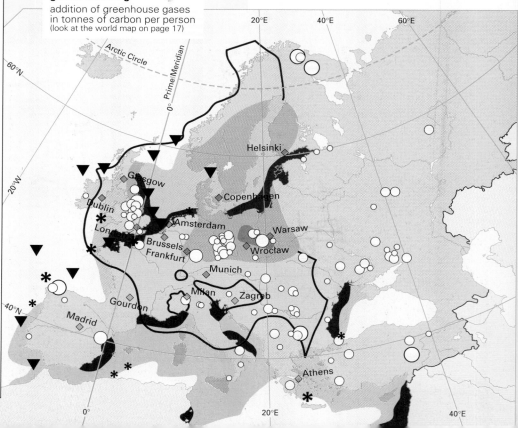

Arctic Circle
Prime Meridian
60°N
20°W
40°N
Helsinki
Glasgow
Copenhagen
Dublin
London
Amsterdam
Warsaw
Brussels
Wrocław
Frankfurt
Munich
Milan
Zagreb
Gourdon
Madrid
Athens
20°E   40°E   60°E
0°   20°E   40°E

Conical Orthomorphic Projection
© Oxford University Press

Population structure of Germany

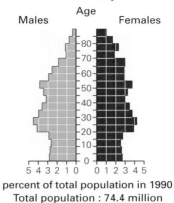

Age

Males | Females

5 4 3 2 1 0 | 0 1 2 3 4 5

percent of total population in 1990
Total population : 74.4 million

Population structure of Greece

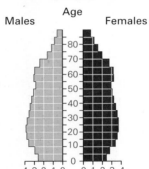

Age

Males | Females

4 3 2 1 0 | 0 1 2 3 4

percent of total population in 1993
Total population : 10.4 million

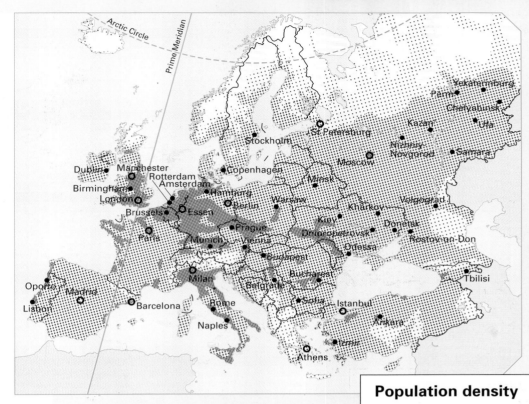

Scale   1: 40 000 000

One centimetre on the map represents
400 kilometres on the ground.

0   400   800   1200 km

Population density

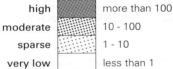

number of people
per square kilometre

high — more than 100
moderate — 10 - 100
sparse — 1 - 10
very low — less than 1

○ major cities and
built up areas of at least
3 million people

● cities with
1 - 3 million people

— country boundary

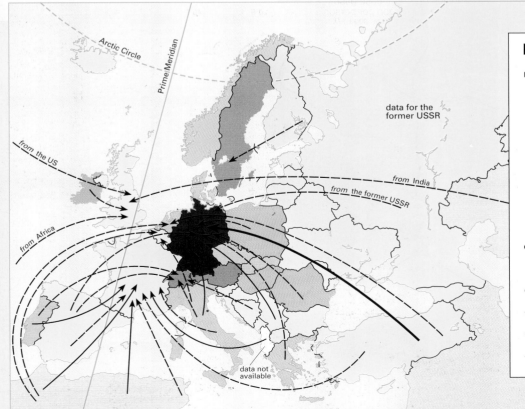

data for the
former USSR

Migration

net total population change due to migration

average annual change
per thousand people, 1986-90

more than 6
3 - 6
gain — 1 - 3
negligible change — 1 to -1
loss — -1 to -8
-8 .02

origin of foreign nationals

people resident in 1990

→ 1 780 000

→ 500 000 - 1 000 000

--→ 100 000 - 500 000

— country boundary

Conical Orthomorphic Projection
© Oxford University Press

48 France

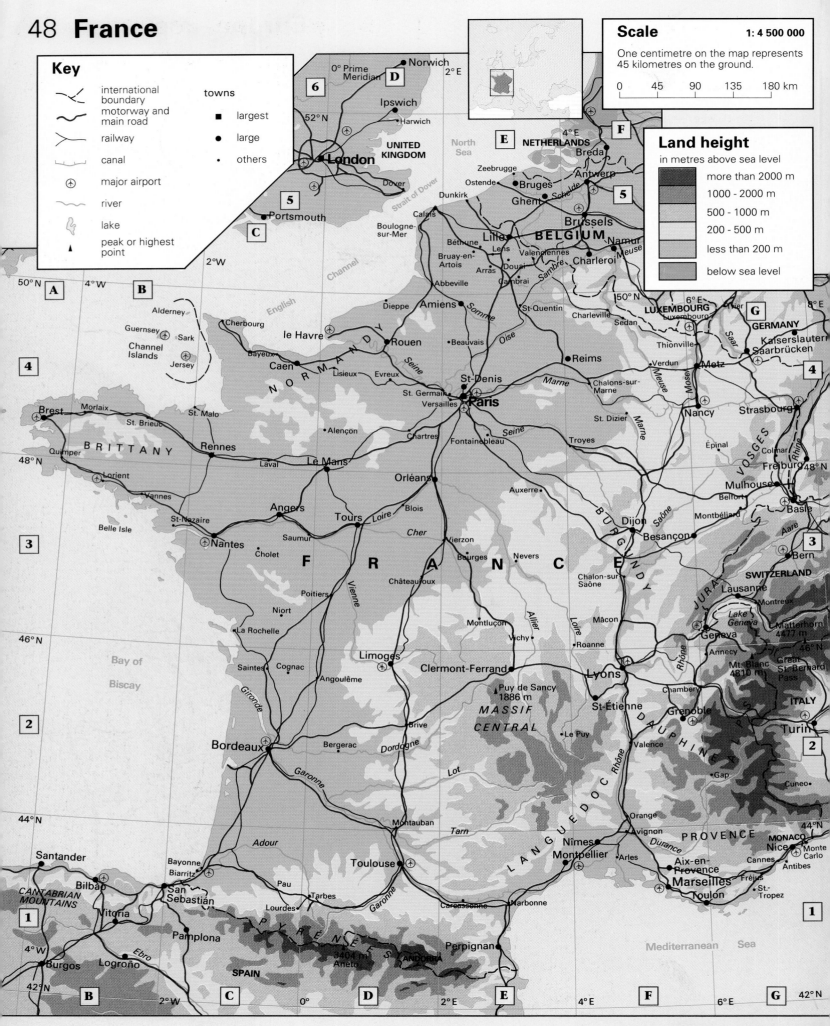

Key

international boundary	towns
motorway and main road	■ largest
railway	● large
canal	· others
⊕ major airport	
river	
lake	
▲ peak or highest point	

Scale

1 : 4 500 000

One centimetre on the map represents 45 kilometres on the ground.

0   45   90   135   180 km

Land height

in metres above sea level

more than 2000 m
1000 - 2000 m
500 - 1000 m
200 - 500 m
less than 200 m
below sea level

Conical Orthomorphic Projection   © Oxford University Press

Benelux, Germany, Alps 49

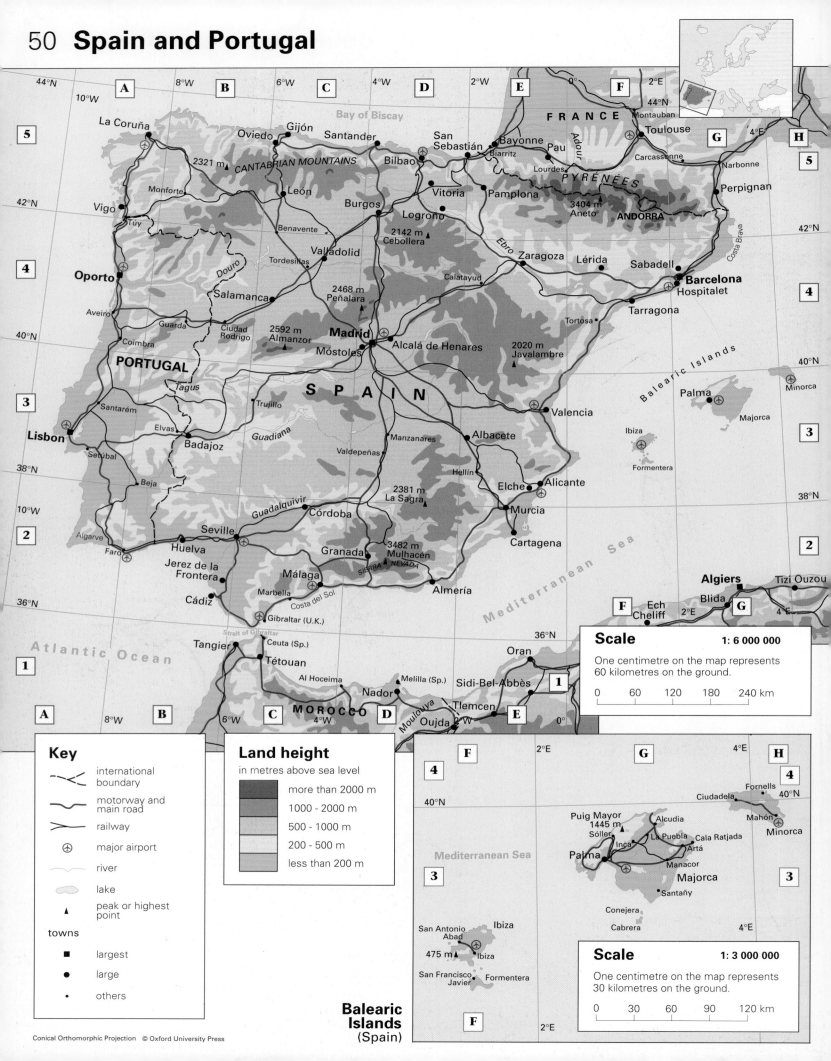

Map of Spain and Portugal

Key

- ⌁ international boundary
- motorway and main road
- railway
- ✈ major airport
- river
- lake
- ▲ peak or highest point

towns
- ■ largest
- ● large
- · others

Land height
in metres above sea level

- more than 2000 m
- 1000 - 2000 m
- 500 - 1000 m
- 200 - 500 m
- less than 200 m

Scale 1: 6 000 000

One centimetre on the map represents 60 kilometres on the ground.

0   60   120   180   240 km

Balearic Islands (Spain)

Scale 1: 3 000 000

One centimetre on the map represents 30 kilometres on the ground.

0   30   60   90   120 km

Conical Orthomorphic Projection   © Oxford University Press

Key

- international boundary
- motorway and main road
- railway
- ⊕ major airport
- river
- lake
- ▲ peak or highest point

towns
- ■ largest
- ● large
- · others

Land height
in metres above sea level

- more than 2000 m
- 1000 - 2000 m
- 500 - 1000 m
- 200 - 500 m
- less than 200 m

Scale
1 : 5 000 000

One centimetre on the map represents 50 kilometres on the ground.

0   50   100   150   200 km

Conical Orthomorphic Projection   © Oxford University Press

Map labels

SWITZERLAND
AUSTRIA
LIECHTENSTEIN
SLOVENIA
CROATIA
BOSNIA-HERZEGOVINA
FRANCE
ALGERIA
TUNISIA
MONACO
MALTA

St. Gallen
Vaduz
Innsbruck
Brenner Pass
Bolzano
Trento
▲3797 m Grossglockner
Graz
Maribor
Villach
Klagenfurt
Kranj
Ljubljana
Zagreb
Varaždin
Karlovac
Sava
Mur
Drava
Inn
Rhine
Lake Constance
Jungfrau 4158 m
Lausanne
Montreux
Lake Geneva
Geneva
Matterhorn 4477 m
St. Moritz
▲4050 m Bernina
Lugano
Lake Maggiore
Lake Como
Como
Lake Garda
4807 m Mont Blanc
Aosta
4807 m
Novara
Milan
Monza
Bérgamo
Bréscia
Verona
Vicenza
Treviso
Udine
Trieste
Rijeka
Istria
Prijedor
Turin
Cuneo
Alessándria
Po
Piacenza
Cremona
Parma
Módena
Bologna
Ferrara
Ravenna
Reggio nell' Emilia
Genoa
La Spézia
Forlí
Rimini
San Marino
Ancona
Split
Nice
Cannes
Antibes
St.-Tropez
MONACO
Prato
Florence
Pisa
Arno
Livorno
Elba
Bastia
Corsica (France)
Ajaccio
Bonifacio
Siena
Arezzo
Perugia
Assisi
Grosseto
Teramo
Terni
Chieti
Pescara
Adriatic Sea
Manfredonia
TIRANË
Tiranë
Rome
Tivoli
Latina
Terracina
Cassino
Fóggia
Barletta
Bari
Monopoli
Bríndisi
Vlorë
1277 m Vesuvius
Naples
Salerno
Potenza
Táranto
Gulf of Táranto
Otranto
Gallipoli
Corfu
Torre del Greco
Sássari
Olbia
Oristano
Sardínia (Italy)
Cágliari
Tyrrhenian Sea
Castrovillari
Rossano
Cosenza
Crotone
Catanzaro
Messina
Reggio di Calábria
Palermo
Marsala
3323 m ▲ Mt. Etna
Sicily
Catánia
Siracusa
Ionian Sea
'Annaba
Tunis
Bizerte
Nabeul
Sousse
Tébessa
Pantelleria (Italy)
Lampedusa (Italy)
Valletta
MALTA
Mediterranean Sea

DOLOMITES
ALPS
APENNINES

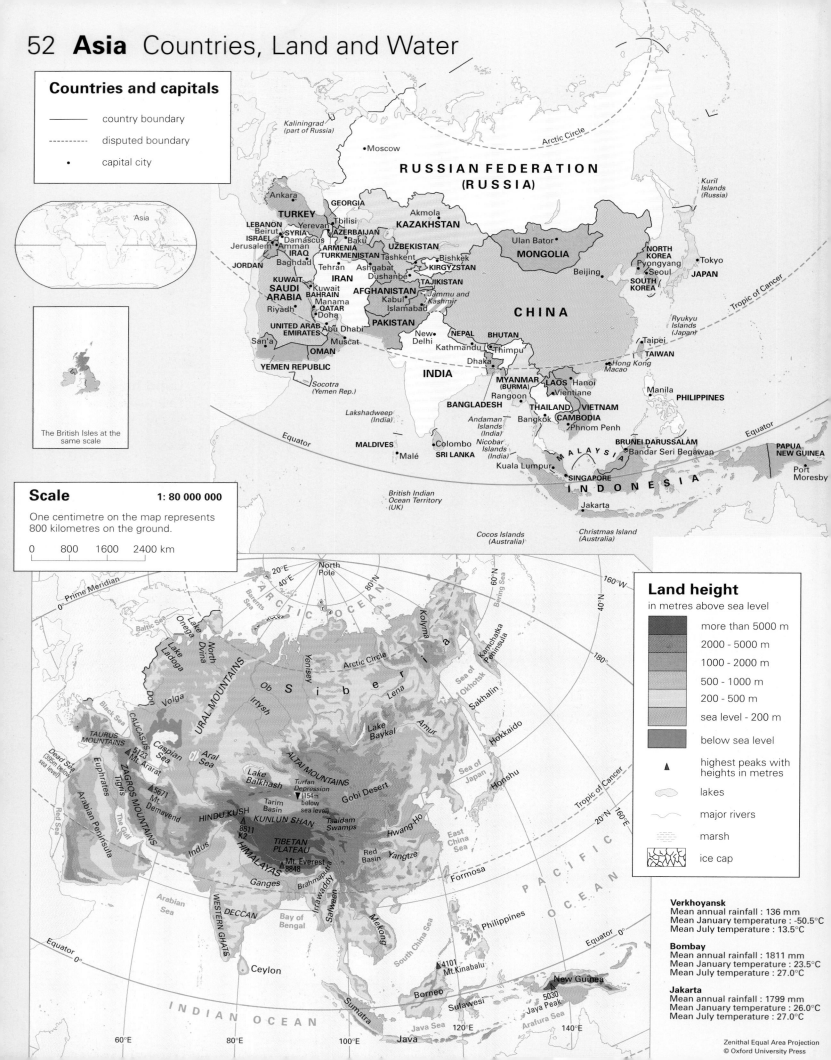

Countries and capitals

———— country boundary

-------- disputed boundary

• capital city

Asia

The British Isles at the same scale

Scale

1: 80 000 000

One centimetre on the map represents 800 kilometres on the ground.

0   800   1600   2400 km

Land height

in metres above sea level

more than 5000 m

2000 - 5000 m

1000 - 2000 m

500 - 1000 m

200 - 500 m

sea level - 200 m

below sea level

▲ highest peaks with heights in metres

lakes

major rivers

marsh

ice cap

Verkhoyansk
Mean annual rainfall : 136 mm
Mean January temperature : -50.5°C
Mean July temperature : 13.5°C

Bombay
Mean annual rainfall : 1811 mm
Mean January temperature : 23.5°C
Mean July temperature : 27.0°C

Jakarta
Mean annual rainfall : 1799 mm
Mean January temperature : 26.0°C
Mean July temperature : 27.0°C

Zenithal Equal Area Projection
© Oxford University Press

Verkhoyansk (100 m)

Temperature in degrees Celsius

Rainfall in millimetres

J F M A M J J A S O N D

Bombay (11 m)

Temperature in degrees Celsius

Rainfall in millimetres

J F M A M J J A S O N D

Jakarta (8 m)

Temperature in degrees Celsius

Rainfall in millimetres

J F M A M J J A S O N D

Climatic regions

Hot tropical rainy
- rain all year
- monsoon
- dry in winter

Very dry
- with no reliable rain
- with a little rain

Influenced by the sea: warm summers, mild winters
- with dry summers (Mediterranean type)
- with dry winters
- with no dry season

Cool
- with dry winters
- rain all year

Cold polar
- no warm season and fairly dry

Mountain
- height of the land strongly affects the climate

Ocean currents
- warm
- cold

Ecosystems

Vegetation types are those which would occur naturally without interference by people

- coniferous forest
- deciduous and mixed forest
- tropical rain forest
- evergreen trees and shrubs
- thorn forest
- temperate grasslands
- semi-desert
- desert
- tundra
- mountains
- country boundary

Scale

1: 80 000 000

One centimetre on the map represents 800 kilometres on the ground.

0   800   1600   2400 km

More information about these ecosystems can be found on page 8.

North Pole
Prime Meridian
Arctic Circle
Tropic of Cancer
Equator
Verkhoyansk
Bombay
Jakarta
typhoons
summer monsoon winds

Zenithal Equal Area Projection
© Oxford University Press

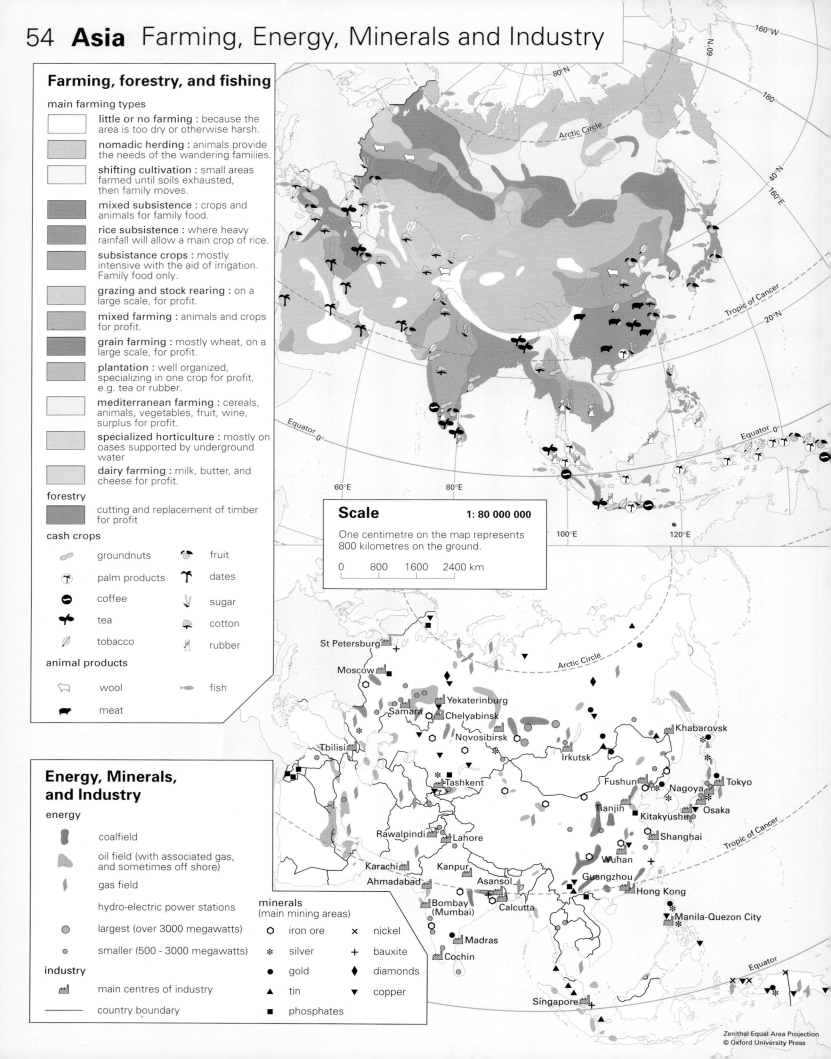

Farming, forestry, and fishing

main farming types

- little or no farming : because the area is too dry or otherwise harsh.
- nomadic herding : animals provide the needs of the wandering families.
- shifting cultivation : small areas farmed until soils exhausted, then family moves.
- mixed subsistence : crops and animals for family food.
- rice subsistence : where heavy rainfall will allow a main crop of rice.
- subsistance crops : mostly intensive with the aid of irrigation. Family food only.
- grazing and stock rearing : on a large scale, for profit.
- mixed farming : animals and crops for profit.
- grain farming : mostly wheat, on a large scale, for profit.
- plantation : well organized, specializing in one crop for profit, e.g. tea or rubber.
- mediterranean farming : cereals, animals, vegetables, fruit, wine, surplus for profit.
- specialized horticulture : mostly on oases supported by underground water
- dairy farming : milk, butter, and cheese for profit.

forestry

- cutting and replacement of timber for profit

cash crops

- groundnuts
- palm products
- coffee
- tea
- tobacco
- fruit
- dates
- sugar
- cotton
- rubber

animal products

- wool
- meat
- fish

Scale   1: 80 000 000

One centimetre on the map represents 800 kilometres on the ground.

0   800   1600   2400 km

Energy, Minerals, and Industry

energy

- coalfield
- oil field (with associated gas, and sometimes off shore)
- gas field
- hydro-electric power stations
  - largest (over 3000 megawatts)
  - smaller (500 - 3000 megawatts)

minerals (main mining areas)

- iron ore
- silver
- gold
- tin
- phosphates
- nickel
- bauxite
- diamonds
- copper

industry

- main centres of industry
- country boundary

St Petersburg
Moscow
Yekaterinburg
Samara
Chelyabinsk
Novosibirsk
Tbilisi
Irkutsk
Khabarovsk
Tashkent
Fushun
Nagoya
Tokyo
Tianjin
Osaka
Kitakyushu
Rawalpindi
Lahore
Shanghai
Karachi
Kanpur
Wuhan
Ahmadabad
Asansol
Guangzhou
Bombay (Mumbai)
Calcutta
Hong Kong
Madras
Manila-Quezon City
Cochin
Singapore

Zenithal Equal Area Projection
© Oxford University Press

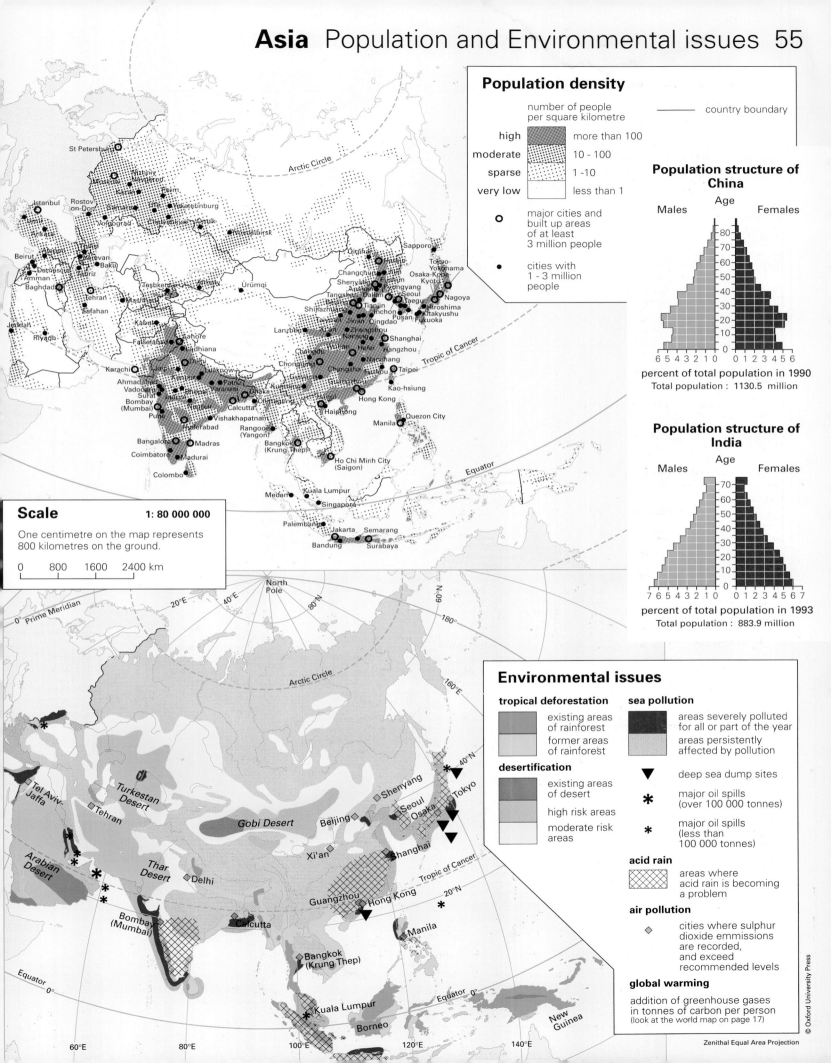

Population density

number of people per square kilometre

— country boundary

		number of people per square kilometre
high		more than 100
moderate		10 - 100
sparse		1 -10
very low		less than 1

○ major cities and built up areas of at least 3 million people

● cities with 1 - 3 million people

Population structure of China

Age

Males — Females

percent of total population in 1990
Total population : 1130.5 million

Population structure of India

Age

Males — Females

percent of total population in 1993
Total population : 883.9 million

Scale

1 : 80 000 000

One centimetre on the map represents 800 kilometres on the ground.

0   800   1600   2400 km

Environmental issues

tropical deforestation

existing areas of rainforest

former areas of rainforest

desertification

existing areas of desert

high risk areas

moderate risk areas

sea pollution

areas severely polluted for all or part of the year

areas persistently affected by pollution

▼ deep sea dump sites

✳ major oil spills (over 100 000 tonnes)

✲ major oil spills (less than 100 000 tonnes)

acid rain

areas where acid rain is becoming a problem

air pollution

◆ cities where sulphur dioxide emmissions are recorded, and exceed recommended levels

global warming

addition of greenhouse gases in tonnes of carbon per person (look at the world map on page 17)

Zenithal Equal Area Projection

© Oxford University Press

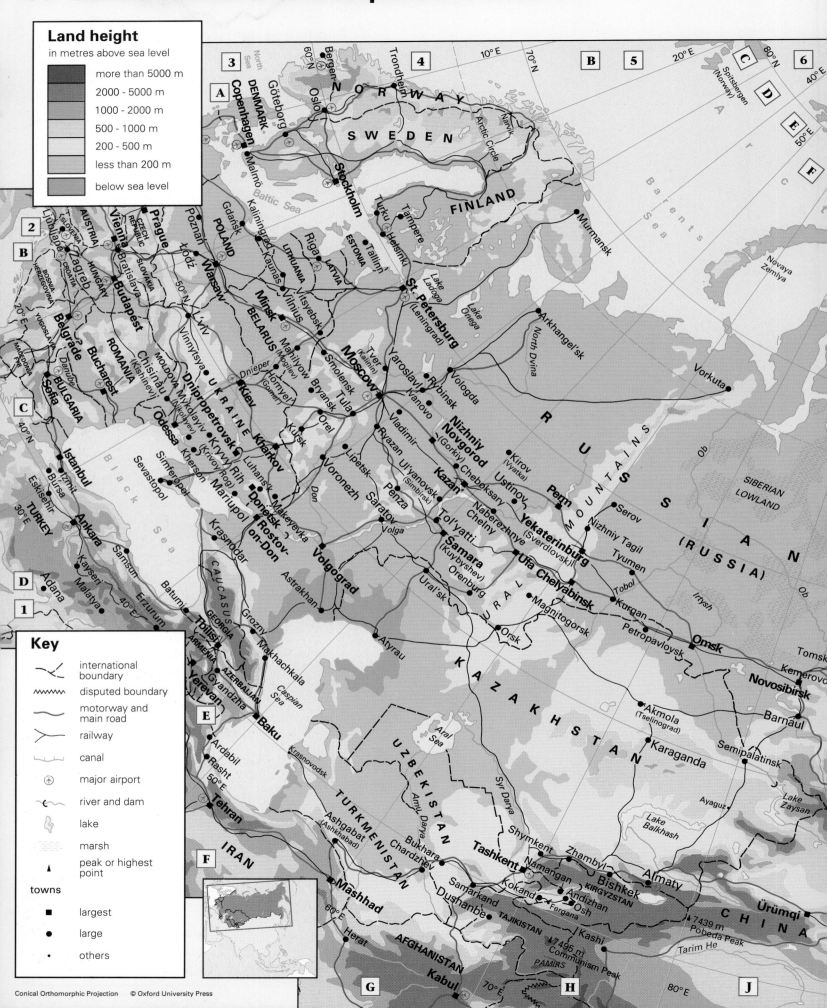

Land height
in metres above sea level

- more than 5000 m
- 2000 - 5000 m
- 1000 - 2000 m
- 500 - 1000 m
- 200 - 500 m
- less than 200 m
- below sea level

Key

- ⌇⌇ international boundary
- ⋀⋀ disputed boundary
- ⌇ motorway and main road
- ⌇ railway
- ⌇ canal
- ✈ major airport
- ⌇ river and dam
- ⌇ lake
- ⌇⌇ marsh
- ▲ peak or highest point

towns

- ■ largest
- ● large
- • others

Conical Orthomorphic Projection   © Oxford University Press

Scale 1: 20 000 000
One centimetre on the map represents
200 kilometres on the ground.

| 0 | 200 | 400 | 600 | 800 km |

Franz Josef
Land

Severnaya
Zemlya

Norilsk

CENTRAL
SIBERIAN
PLATEAU

Yenisey

Verkhoyansk

Lena

Yakutsk

Magadan

Kamchatka
Peninsula

Petropavlovsk-
Kamchatskiy

Sea of
Okhotsk

Kuril
Islands

FEDERATION

Angara

Lena

Tynda

Ust-Kut

Krasnoyarsk

Bratsk

Komsomolsk-
on-Amur

Sovetskaya
Gavan

Sakhalin

Amur

Novokuznetsk

Lake
Baykal

Blagoveshchensk

Khabarovsk

Shilka

Irkutsk

Chita

Ulan-Ude

Hegang

Jiamusi

Qiqihar

Jixi

Lake
Khanka

Harbin

Vladivostok

Ulan Bator

Kerulen

Mudanjiang

Jilin

Changchun

Chongjin

Sea of
Japan

ALTAI
MOUNTAINS

4226 m

MONGOLIA

CHINA

Shenyang

Anshan

Fushun

NORTH KOREA

Sendai

JAPAN
Tokyo

Hami

GOBI DESERT

Pyongyang

Seoul

SOUTH
KOREA

Kyoto

Nagoya

Osaka

Hohhot

Beijing
(Peking)

Dalian

New Siberian
Islands

Wrangel
Island

Arctic Circle

Bering
Sea

Bering Strait

U.S.A.

St.
Lawrence

Kolyma

Sapporo

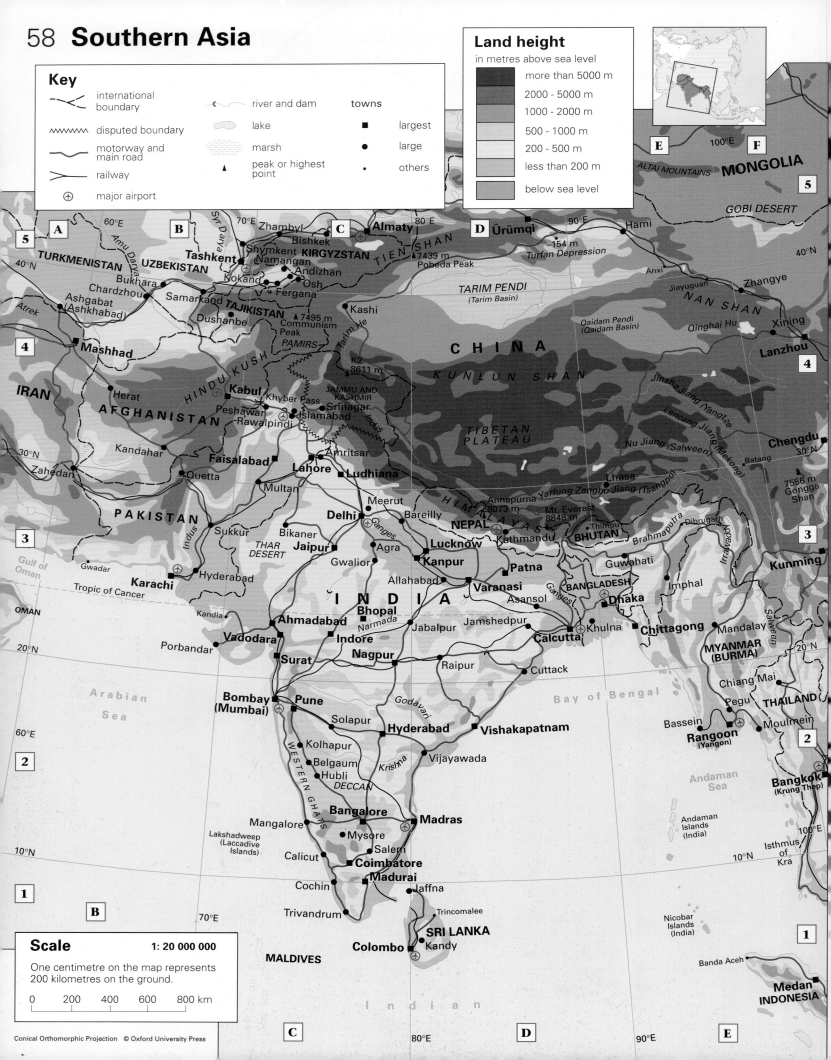

© Oxford University Press

Key

international boundary	
motorway and main road	
railway	
canal	
major airport	✈
river and dam	
lake	
marsh	
peak or highest point	▲

towns
- ■ largest
- ● large
- · others

Land height

in metres above sea level

- more than 5000 m
- 2000 - 5000 m
- 1000 - 2000 m
- 500 - 1000 m
- 200 - 500 m
- less than 200 m

Scale (China) 1: 20 000 000

One centimetre on the map represents 200 kilometres on the ground.

0   200   400   600   800 km

Scale (Japan) 1: 10 000 000

One centimetre on the map represents 100 kilometres on the ground.

0   100   200   300   400 km

Zenithal Equidistant Projection

Conical Orthomorphic Projection

Japan labels

HOKKAIDO, HONSHU, SHIKOKU, KYUSHU, JAPAN

Wakkanai, Nemuro, Obihiro, Kushiro, Asahikawa, Mt. Asahi 2290 m, Sapporo, Muroran, Hakodate, Ishikari, Tsugaru Channel, Aomori, Hachinohe, Moroka, Morioka, Kitakami, Sendai, Akita, Yamagata, Fukushima, Sado, Niigata, Utsunomiya, Chiba, TOKYO, Yokohama, Mt. Fuji 3776 m, Shizuoka, Hamamatsu, Izu Islands, Tone, Iwaki, Koriyama, Nagoya, Yokkaichi, Matsuzaka, Gifu, Fukui, Kanazawa, Toyama, KYOTO, Kobe, OSAKA, Wakayama, Lake Biwa, Himeji, Okayama, Takamatsu, Kochi, Tottori, Matsue, Matsuyama, Oki Islands, Inland Sea, Hiroshima, Shimonoseki, KITAKYUSHU, Fukuoka, Oita, Miyazaki, Kumamoto, Nagasaki, Kagoshima, Osumi Islands, Sea of Japan, Pacific Ocean, Ryukyu Islands, Tropic of Cancer

China / Korea / SE Asia labels

RUSSIA, MONGOLIA, GOBI DESERT, NAN SHAN, CHINA, Qaidam Pendi (Qaidam Basin), Sichuan Pendi (Sichuan Basin)

Hegang, Jiamusi, Harbin, Jilin, Qiqihar, Mudanjiang, Lake Khanka, Vladivostok, Nen Jiang, Changchun, Fushun, Shenyang, Anshan, Benxi, Jixi, Guli, Songhua, Liao He, Tangshan, Dalian, Zhangjiakou, Beijing (Peking), Tianjin, Hohhot, Baotou, Taiyuan, Shijiazhuang, Zibo, Jinan (Tsinan), Qingdao, Lianyungang, Xuzhou, Huang He, Great Wall, Yinchuan, Lanzhou, Zhangye, Zhangye, Jiayuguan, Anxi, Xining, Qinghai Hu, Wei He, Xi'an, Luoyang, Zhengzhou, Kaifeng, Huainan, Hefei, Nanjing, Suzhou, Tai Hu, Shanghai, Hangzhou, Chang Jiang (Yangtze), Wuhan, Nanchang, Poyang Hu, Dongting Hu, Changsha, Chongqing, Chengdu, Jinsha Jiang (Yangtze), Gongga Shan 7556 m, Guiyang, Kunming, Guiyang, Liuzhou, Guangzhou (Canton), Hong Kong, Macao, Fuzhou, Zhanjiang, Xi Jiang, Nanning, Hainan, Taipei, TAIWAN, Kao-hsiung, South China Sea

NORTH KOREA, SOUTH KOREA, Chongjin, Hungnam, Wonsan, Pyongyang, Nampo, Kaesong, Seoul, Inchon, Taejon, Taegu, Pusan, Kwangju, Yellow Sea, Ullung Island (South Korea)

VIETNAM, LAOS, CAMBODIA, THAILAND, MYANMAR (BURMA), ANNAM RANGE

Hanoi, Haiphong, Vinh, Hue, Da Nang, Qui Nhon, Nha-Trang, Ho Chi Minh City (Saigon), Phnom Penh, Kratie, Bangkok (Krung Thep), Vientiane, Luang Prabang, Chiang Mai, Moulmein, Mekong, Song Koi, Salween, Menam, Irrawaddy, Gulf of Thailand, Nu Jiang, Lancang Jiang (Mekong)

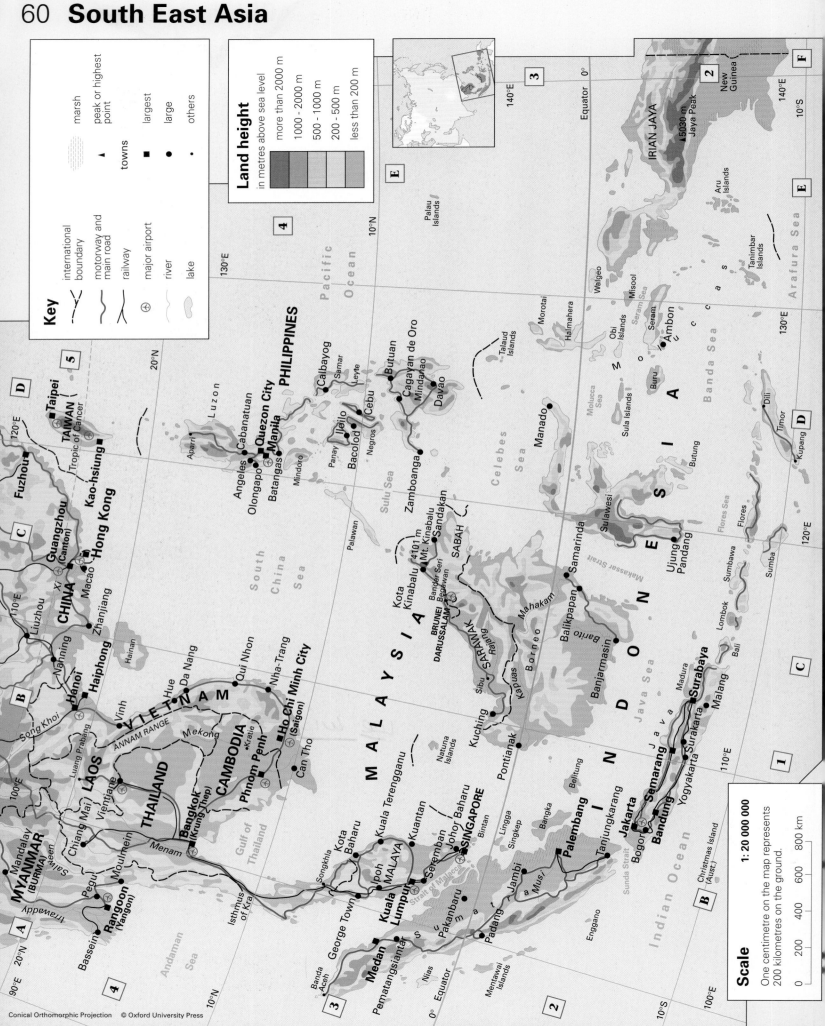

Key

towns
- ▲ peak or highest point
- ■ largest
- ● large
- · others

- marsh

- --- international boundary
- motorway and main road
- railway
- ⊕ major airport
- river
- lake

Land height
in metres above sea level

- more than 2000 m
- 1000 - 2000 m
- 500 - 1000 m
- 200 - 500 m
- less than 200 m

Scale
1: 20 000 000

One centimetre on the map represents
200 kilometres on the ground.

0 200 400 600 800 km

Conical Orthomorphic Projection   © Oxford University Press

CHINA
Fuzhou
Guangzhou (Canton)
Xi
Macao
Hong Kong
Liuzhou
Nanning
Zhanjiang
Hainan
Liuzhou

Taipei
TAIWAN
Kao-hsiung
Tropic of Cancer

Hanoi
Haiphong
VIETNAM
Vinh
Song Khoi
Luang Prabang
Vientiane
LAOS
ANNAM RANGE
Da Nang
Hue
Qui Nhon
Nha-Trang
Ho Chi Minh City (Saigon)
Can Tho
Mekong
Kratie
CAMBODIA
Phnom Penh
THAILAND
Bangkok (Krung Thep)
Chiang Mai
Menam
Gulf of Thailand

MYANMAR (BURMA)
Mandalay
Salween
Pegu
Moulmein
Rangoon (Yangon)
Bassein
Irrawaddy
Andaman Sea
Isthmus of Kra

PHILIPPINES
Luzon
Aparri
Cabanatuan
Angeles
Quezon City
Manila
Olongapo
Batangas
Mindoro
Calbayog
Samar
Leyte
Iloilo
Panay
Bacolod
Negros
Cebu
Butuan
Cagayan de Oro
Mindanao
Davao
Zamboanga
Palawan

Sulu Sea
South China Sea
Pacific Ocean
Palau Islands

MALAYSIA
Kota Kinabalu
Mt. Kinabalu 4101 m
Sandakan
SABAH
BRUNEI DARUSSALAM
Bandar Seri Begawan
SARAWAK
Rajang
Sibu
Kuching
Borneo
Kapuas
Pontianak
Natuna Islands
Mahakam
Samarinda
Balikpapan
Barito
Banjarmasin

Kuala Terengganu
Kuantan
Kota Baharu
Songkhla
George Town
MALAYA
Ipoh
Kuala Lumpur
Seremban
Johor Baharu
SINGAPORE
Bintan
Lingga
Singkep
Bangka
Medan
Pematangsiantar
Pakanbaru
Jambi
Musi
Padang
Palembang
Tanjungkarang
Sunda Strait
Mentawai Islands
Nias
Banda Aceh
Strait of Malacca

INDONESIA
Jakarta
Bogor
Bandung
Semarang
Surakarta
Yogyakarta
Java
Surabaya
Malang
Madura
Bali
Lombok
Sumbawa
Flores Sea
Flores
Sumba
Java Sea

Celebes Sea
Manado
Sulawesi
Ujung Pandang
Makassar Strait
Butung
Buru
Obi Islands
Sula Islands
Molucca Sea
Morotai
Halmahera
Talaud Islands
Seram
Ambon
Banda Sea
Seram Sea
Buru
Misool
Waigeo
Tanimbar Islands
Aru Islands
IRIAN JAYA
New Guinea
Java Peak 5030 m
Arafura Sea
Timor
Dili
Kupang

Indian Ocean
Christmas Island (Aust.)
Enggano

Equator
Tropic of Cancer
10°N
20°N
10°S
90°E 100°E 110°E 120°E 130°E 140°E

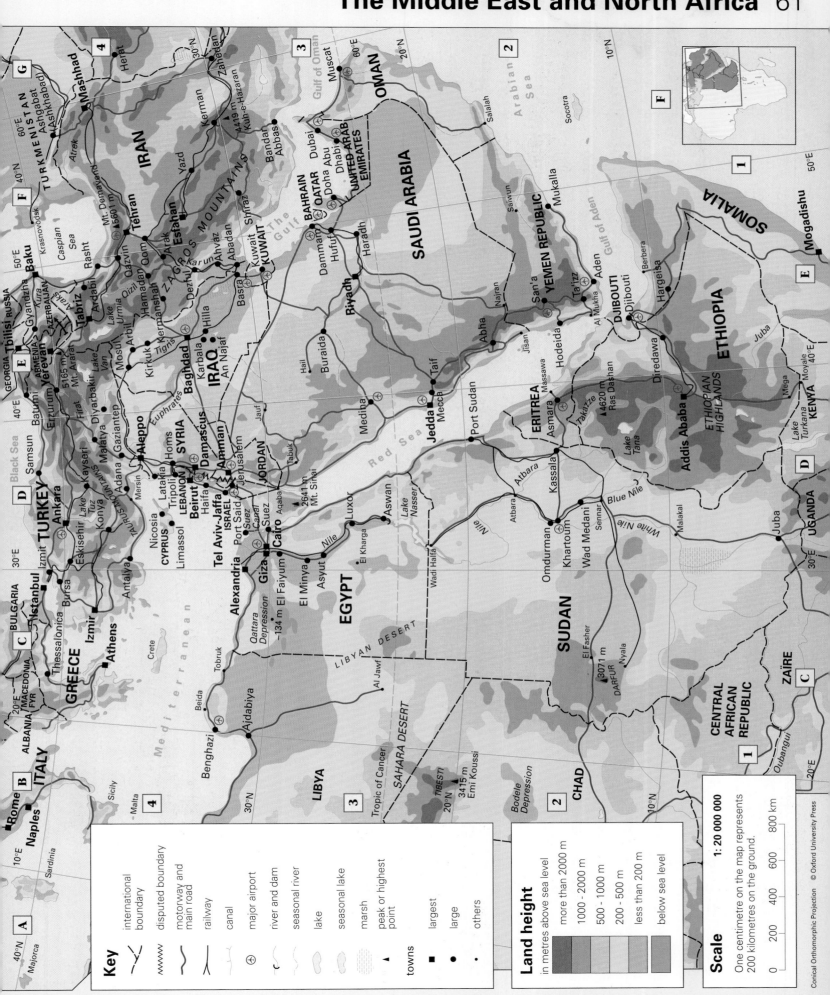

Key

	international boundary
	disputed boundary
⌒⌒⌒	motorway and main road
	railway
	canal
⊕	major airport
	river and dam
	seasonal river
	lake
	seasonal lake
	marsh
▲	peak or highest point

towns

■	largest
●	large
•	others

Land height

in metres above sea level

	more than 2000 m
	1000 - 2000 m
	500 - 1000 m
	200 - 500 m
	less than 200 m
	below sea level

Scale   1: 20 000 000

One centimetre on the map represents
200 kilometres on the ground.

0	200	400	600	800 km

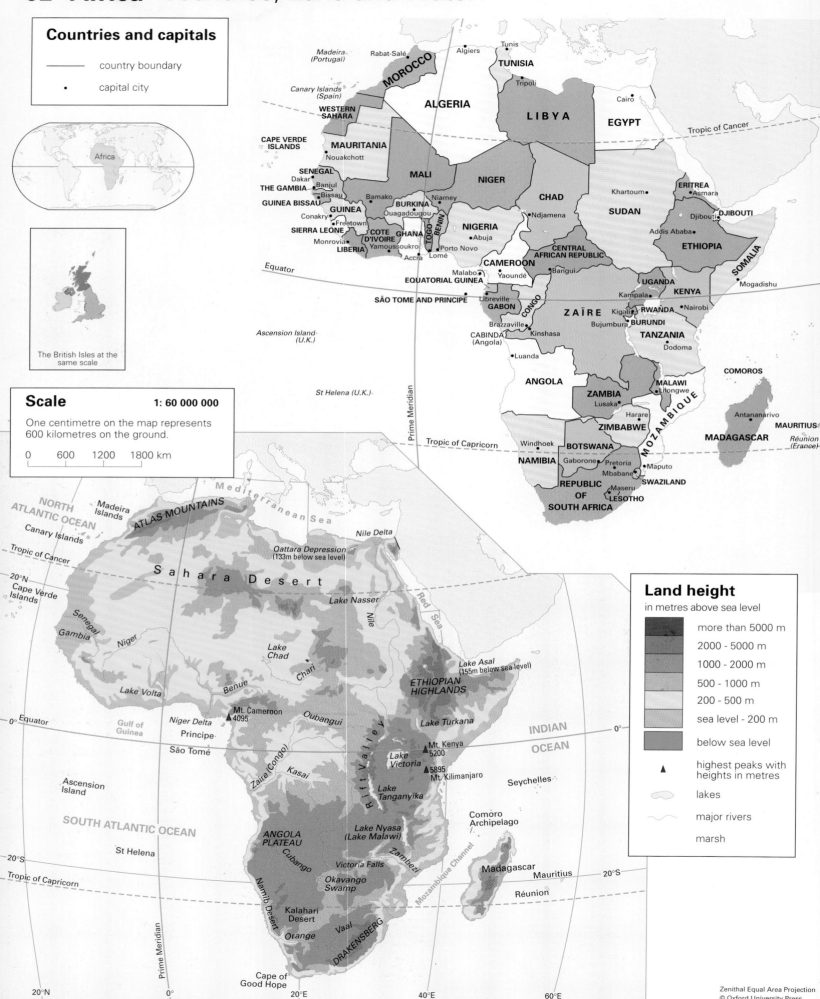

Countries and capitals

— country boundary

• capital city

Africa

The British Isles at the same scale

Scale

1: 60 000 000

One centimetre on the map represents 600 kilometres on the ground.

0   600   1200   1800 km

MOROCCO Rabat-Salé
Madeira (Portugal)
Tunis
TUNISIA Tripoli
Algiers
ALGERIA
Canary Islands (Spain)
WESTERN SAHARA
LIBYA
EGYPT Cairo
Tropic of Cancer
CAPE VERDE ISLANDS
MAURITANIA Nouakchott
MALI Bamako
NIGER Niamey
CHAD Ndjamena
Khartoum
ERITREA Asmara
DJIBOUTI Djibouti
SENEGAL Dakar
THE GAMBIA Banjul
Bissau
GUINEA BISSAU
BURKINA Ouagadougou
SUDAN
Addis Ababa
GUINEA Conakry
Freetown
SIERRA LEONE Monrovia
COTE D'IVOIRE
GHANA Yamoussoukro
TOGO **BENIN**
NIGERIA Abuja
Porto Novo
Lomé
Accra
ETHIOPIA
SOMALIA
LIBERIA
CAMEROON Yaoundé
CENTRAL AFRICAN REPUBLIC Bangui
Malabo
EQUATORIAL GUINEA
UGANDA Kampala
KENYA Nairobi
Mogadishu
SÃO TOME AND PRINCIPE
Libreville
GABON
CONGO
ZAÏRE Kigali
RWANDA Bujumbura
BURUNDI
Brazzaville
CABINDA (Angola) Kinshasa
TANZANIA Dodoma
Luanda
COMOROS
ANGOLA
MALAWI Lilongwe
ZAMBIA Lusaka
MOZAMBIQUE
Antananarivo
MAURITIUS
Harare
ZIMBABWE Windhoek
MADAGASCAR
Réunion (France)
BOTSWANA Gaborone
NAMIBIA Pretoria
Maputo
Mbabane
SWAZILAND
REPUBLIC OF SOUTH AFRICA Maseru
LESOTHO
Equator
St Helena (U.K.)
Ascension Island (U.K.)
Prime Meridian
Tropic of Capricorn

NORTH ATLANTIC OCEAN
Madeira Islands
Canary Islands
Tropic of Cancer
20°N
Cape Verde Islands
Senegal
Gambia
Niger
Mediterranean Sea
ATLAS MOUNTAINS
Nile Delta
Qattara Depression (133m below sea level)
S a h a r a   D e s e r t
Lake Nasser
Nile
Red Sea
Lake Chad
Chari
Benue
Lake Asal (155m below sea level)
ETHIOPIAN HIGHLANDS
Mt. Cameroon 4095
Niger Delta
Principe
São Tomé
Oubangui
Zaire (Congo)
Kasai
Gulf of Guinea
Ascension Island
SOUTH ATLANTIC OCEAN
Lake Volta
0° Equator
Lake Turkana
INDIAN OCEAN 0°
Mt. Kenya 5200
Lake Victoria
Rift Valley
5895 Mt. Kilimanjaro
Seychelles
Lake Tanganyika
Comoro Archipelago
ANGOLA PLATEAU
Lake Nyasa (Lake Malawi)
Victoria Falls
Zambezi
Madagascar
Mauritius
20°S
St Helena
Cubango
Namib Desert
Okavango Swamp
Mozambique Channel
Réunion
Tropic of Capricorn
Kalahari Desert
Vaal
DRAKENSBERG
Orange
Cape of Good Hope
20°N   0°   20°E   40°E   60°E
Prime Meridian

Land height

in metres above sea level

- more than 5000 m
- 2000 – 5000 m
- 1000 – 2000 m
- 500 – 1000 m
- 200 – 500 m
- sea level – 200 m
- below sea level

▲ highest peaks with heights in metres

lakes

major rivers

marsh

Zenithal Equal Area Projection
© Oxford University Press

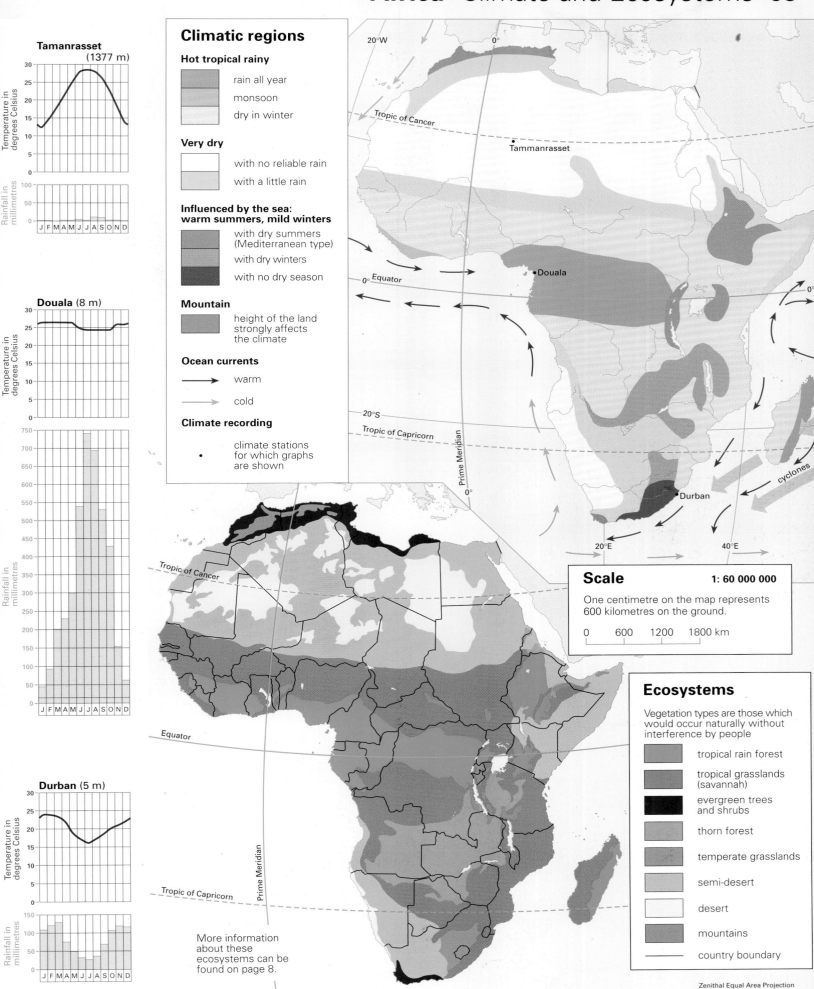

Tamanrasset (1377 m)

Temperature in degrees Celsius

Rainfall in millimetres

J F M A M J J A S O N D

Douala (8 m)

Temperature in degrees Celsius

Rainfall in millimetres

J F M A M J J A S O N D

Durban (5 m)

Temperature in degrees Celsius

Rainfall in millimetres

J F M A M J J A S O N D

Climatic regions

Hot tropical rainy

- rain all year
- monsoon
- dry in winter

Very dry

- with no reliable rain
- with a little rain

Influenced by the sea: warm summers, mild winters

- with dry summers (Mediterranean type)
- with dry winters
- with no dry season

Mountain

- height of the land strongly affects the climate

Ocean currents

→ warm

→ cold

Climate recording

- climate stations for which graphs are shown

20°W 0°

Tropic of Cancer

• Tammanrasset

0° Equator

• Douala

20°S

Tropic of Capricorn

Prime Meridian

0°

0°

cyclones

Durban

20°E 40°E

Scale 1: 60 000 000

One centimetre on the map represents 600 kilometres on the ground.

0 600 1200 1800 km

Tropic of Cancer

Equator

Prime Meridian

Tropic of Capricorn

More information about these ecosystems can be found on page 8.

Ecosystems

Vegetation types are those which would occur naturally without interference by people

- tropical rain forest
- tropical grasslands (savannah)
- evergreen trees and shrubs
- thorn forest
- temperate grasslands
- semi-desert
- desert
- mountains
- —— country boundary

Zenithal Equal Area Projection
© Oxford University Press

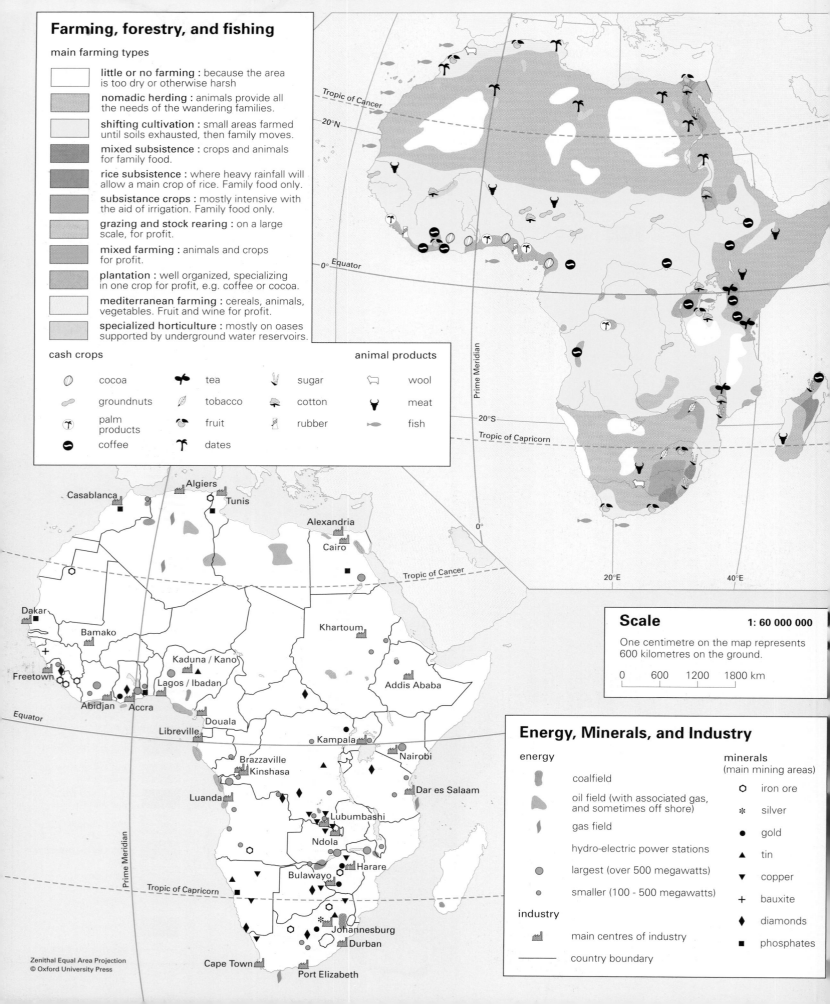

Farming, forestry, and fishing

main farming types

- **little or no farming** : because the area is too dry or otherwise harsh
- **nomadic herding** : animals provide all the needs of the wandering families.
- **shifting cultivation** : small areas farmed until soils exhausted, then family moves.
- **mixed subsistence** : crops and animals for family food.
- **rice subsistence** : where heavy rainfall will allow a main crop of rice. Family food only.
- **subsistance crops** : mostly intensive with the aid of irrigation. Family food only.
- **grazing and stock rearing** : on a large scale, for profit.
- **mixed farming** : animals and crops for profit.
- **plantation** : well organized, specializing in one crop for profit, e.g. coffee or cocoa.
- **mediterranean farming** : cereals, animals, vegetables. Fruit and wine for profit.
- **specialized horticulture** : mostly on oases supported by underground water reservoirs.

cash crops

- cocoa
- groundnuts
- palm products
- coffee
- tea
- tobacco
- fruit
- dates
- sugar
- cotton
- rubber
- wool
- meat
- fish

animal products

Zenithal Equal Area Projection
© Oxford University Press

Energy, Minerals, and Industry

energy

- coalfield
- oil field (with associated gas, and sometimes off shore)
- gas field
- hydro-electric power stations
  - largest (over 500 megawatts)
  - smaller (100 - 500 megawatts)

industry

- main centres of industry
- country boundary

minerals
(main mining areas)

- iron ore
- silver
- gold
- tin
- copper
- bauxite
- diamonds
- phosphates

Scale   1: 60 000 000

One centimetre on the map represents 600 kilometres on the ground.

0   600   1200   1800 km

Place names: Casablanca, Algiers, Tunis, Alexandria, Cairo, Dakar, Bamako, Freetown, Kaduna / Kano, Lagos / Ibadan, Abidjan, Accra, Khartoum, Addis Ababa, Douala, Libreville, Kampala, Nairobi, Brazzaville, Kinshasa, Dar es Salaam, Luanda, Lubumbashi, Ndola, Harare, Bulawayo, Johannesburg, Durban, Cape Town, Port Elizabeth

Population structure of Kenya

Age
Males — Females

80
70
60
50
40
30
20
10

9 8 7 6 5 4 3 2 1 0   0 1 2 3 4 5 6 7 8 9

percent of total population in 1989
Total population : 21.4 million

Population structure of Egypt

Age
Males — Females

70
60
50
40
30
20
10
0

8 7 6 5 4 3 2 1 0   0 1 2 3 4 5 6 7 8

percent of total population in 1992
Total population : 55.2 million

Population density

number of people per square kilometre

high	more than 100
moderate	10 - 100
sparse	1 - 10
very low	less than 1

○ major cities and built up areas of at least 3 million people

● cities with 1 - 3 million people

—— country boundary

Scale   1: 60 000 000

One centimetre on the map represents 600 kilometres on the ground.

0   600   1200   1800 km

Rabat-Salé
Casablanca
Algiers
Tunis
Alexandria
Giza Cairo
Tropic of Cancer
Dakar
Addis Ababa
Abidjan Lagos
Mogadishu
Equator
Kinshasa
Nairobi
Dar es Salaam
Luanda
Harare
Antananarivo
Tropic of Capricorn
Pretoria
Maputo
Johannesburg
Durban
Cape Town

Prime Meridian

Environmental issues

tropical deforestation

existing areas of rainforest

former areas of rainforest

desertification

existing areas of desert

high risk areas

moderate risk areas

sea pollution

areas severely polluted for all or part of the year

areas persistently affected by pollution

▼ deep sea dump sites

✳ major oil spills (over 100 000 tonnes)

∗ major oil spills (less than 100 000 tonnes)

acid rain

areas where acid rain is becoming a problem

tsetse fly

areas affected by the tsetse fly

Tropic of Cancer
20°N
Sahara Desert
S a h e l
Somali Desert
0° Equator
Congo Basin
20°S
Tropic of Capricorn
Namib Desert
Madagascar
Kalahari Desert
Prime Meridian
20°W
0°
20°E
40°E

global warming
addition of greenhouse gases in tonnes of carbon per person
(look at the world map on page 17)

Zenithal Equal Area Projection
© Oxford University Press

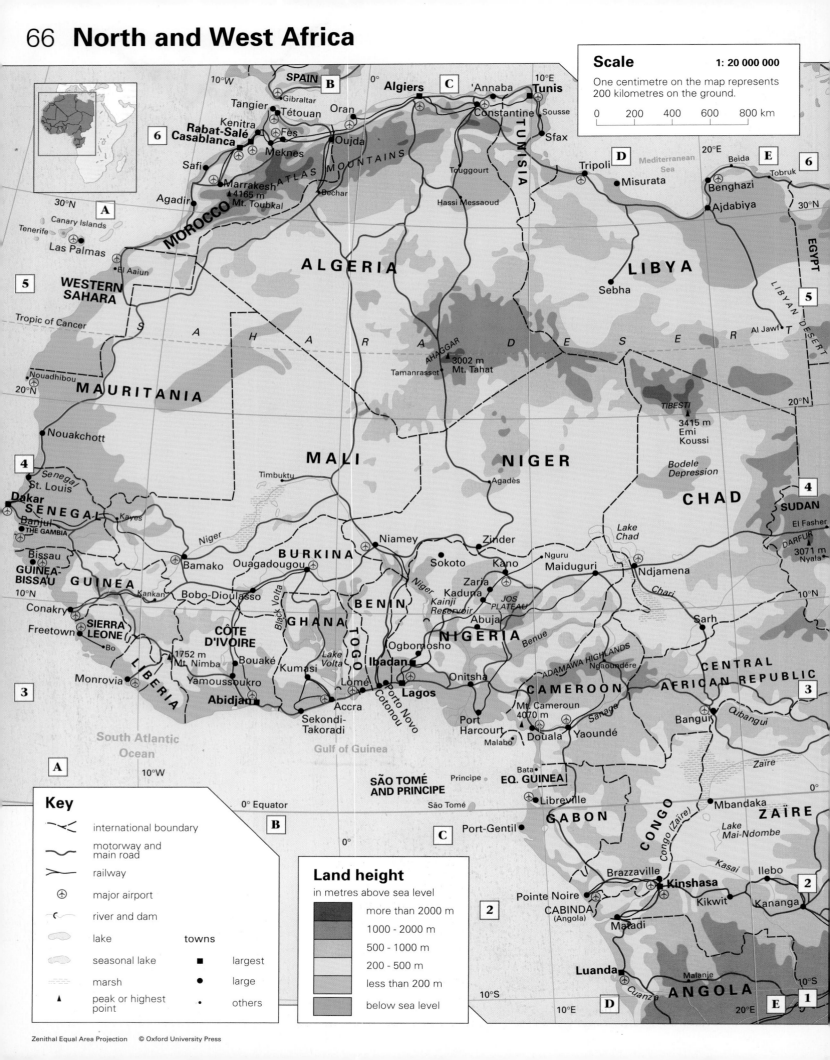

Scale
1: 20 000 000
One centimetre on the map represents 200 kilometres on the ground.

0   200   400   600   800 km

Key

international boundary	
motorway and main road	
railway	
⊕	major airport
	river and dam
	lake
	seasonal lake
	marsh
▲	peak or highest point

towns

■	largest
●	large
·	others

Land height
in metres above sea level

	more than 2000 m
	1000 - 2000 m
	500 - 1000 m
	200 - 500 m
	less than 200 m
	below sea level

Zenithal Equal Area Projection   © Oxford University Press

B 20°E C El Fasher 30°E Wad Medani D 40°E ERITREA E Gulf of Aden 50°E 6

6

CHAD
Sennar
Ras Dashan ▲4620 m
DJIBOUTI
Djibouti
10°N

Chari
▲3071 m
DARFUR
Nyala
SUDAN
White Nile
Blue Nile
Lake Tana
ETHIOPIA
Addis Ababa
ETHIOPIAN HIGHLANDS
Diredawa
Berbera
Hargeisa

NIGERIA 10°E
Sarh
Benue
Ngaoundéré
ADAMAWA HIGHLANDS
CENTRAL
AFRICAN REPUBLIC
Juba
Malakal
SOMALIA
5

5

CAMEROON
Douala
Sanaga
Yaoundé
Bangui
Oubangui
Uele
Lake Turkana
Mega
Moyale
Mogadishu
Equator 0°

EQ. GUINEA
Bata
Zaïre
Kisangani
Mbandaka
Boyoma Falls
Lake Mobutu
Mt. Ruwenzori 5118 m
Lake Edward
UGANDA
Kampala
Entebbe
Lake Kyoga
Kisumu
KENYA
5199 m
Mt. Kenya
Nairobi
4

4

GABON
CONGO
Lake Mai-Ndombe
ZAÏRE
Lualaba
Lake Kivu
Bukavu
RWANDA
Kigali
Lake Victoria
5895 m
Mt. Kilimanjaro
Mombasa
Indian
Ocean

Brazzaville
Pointe Noire
Kasai
Ilebo
Congo (Zaïre)
Bujumbura
BURUNDI
Kigoma
Mwanza
TANZANIA
Tabora
Tanga
Zanzibar

CABINDA (Angola)
Kinshasa
Kikwit
Kananga
Mbuji-Mayi
Kalemie
Lake Tanganyika
Dodoma
Dar es Salaam

Matadi

Luanda
Malanje
Cuanza
Lake Mweru
Lake Rukwa
WESTERN RIFT VALLEY
EASTERN RIFT VALLEY
Aldabra Islands
10°S

Lobito
Benguela
Huambo
Kasai
Lake Bangweulu
Lake Nyasa (Lake Malawi)
Ruvuma
COMOROS
Moroni

ANGOLA
Lubango
Likasi
Lubumbashi
Kitwe
Ndola
Kabwe
MALAWI
Lilongwe
Nampula
Mozambique
Mahajanga
3

3

Cunene
Cubango
Zambezi
ZAMBIA
Lusaka
Lake Cabora Bassa
Blantyre
MOZAMBIQUE
Toamasina

NAMIBIA
Etosha Pan
Okavango Swamp
Victoria Falls
ZIMBABWE
Harare
Lake Kariba
Zambezi
Beira
Antananarivo
20°S

Walvis Bay
Windhoek
KALAHARI DESERT
Bulawayo
Europa
MADAGASCAR

NAMIB DESERT
BOTSWANA
Limpopo
Tropic of Capricorn
Toliara
2

2

Lüderitz
Gaborone
Pretoria
Johannesburg
Mbabane
Maputo
SWAZILAND
40°E
50°E

Atlantic Ocean
Orange
Kimberley
Bloemfontein
Vaal
HIGH VELD
Maseru
3482 m
DRAKENSBERG
LESOTHO
Pietermaritzburg
Durban
E
30°S

REPUBLIC OF SOUTH AFRICA
GREAT KARROO
East London
1

1

Cape Town
Cape of Good Hope
Port Elizabeth

A 10°E B 20°E C 30°E D

Scale 1: 20 000 000

One centimetre on the map represents 200 kilometres on the ground.

0   200   400   600   800 km

For explanations of the symbols and colours used on this map look at the oppsite page.

Zenithal Equal Area Projection   © Oxford University Press

Countries and capitals

— country boundary
• capital city

Oceania

The British Isles at the same scale

Darwin (30 m)

Temperature in degrees Celsius

Rainfall in millimetres

J F M A M J J A S O N D

IRIAN JAYA
(part of Indonesia)

PAPUA NEW GUINEA

SOLOMON ISLANDS

Port Moresby

Honiara

VANUATU

Vila

New Caledonia
(France)

Nouméa

AUSTRALIA

Tropic of Capricorn

Equator

Norfolk Island
(Australia)

Lord Howe Island
(Australia)

• Canberra

NEW ZEALAND

Wellington

Scale

1 : 44 000 000

One centimetre on the map represents
440 kilometres on the ground.

0   440   880   1320 km

Darwin
Mean annual rainfall : 1492 mm
Mean January temperature : 28.5°C
Mean July temperature : 26.0°C

Alice Springs
Mean annual rainfall : 253 mm
Mean January temperature : 28.5°C
Mean July temperature : 11.5°C

Christchurch
Mean annual rainfall : 637mm
Mean January temperature : 16.5°C
Mean July temperature : 67.0°C

Land height
in metres above sea level

- more than 2000 m
- 1000 - 2000 m
- 500 - 1000 m
- 200 - 500 m
- sea level - 200 m
- below sea level
- ▲ highest peaks with heights in metres
- lakes
- major rivers
- major seasonal rivers
- coral reef

120°E

140°E

Equator   0°

0° Equator

Jaya Peak 5030 ▲

New Guinea

Bismarck Sea

New Ireland

New Britain

4508▲ Mt. Wilhelm

Bougainville Island

160°E

Solomon Islands

Santa Cruz Islands

Arafura Sea

Timor Sea

Arnham Land

Gulf of Carpentaria

Cape York Peninsula

Great Barrier Reef

Coral Sea

Espiritu Santo

INDIAN OCEAN

Great Sandy Desert

MACDONNELL RANGES

Flinders

GREAT DIVIDING RANGE

New Caledonia

Loyalty Islands

20°S

Tropic of Capricorn

PACIFIC OCEAN

20°S

HAMERSLEY RANGE

Mt Meharry ▲1251

Gibson Desert

Simpson Desert

▲867 Ayers Rock

Sturt Desert

Tropic of Capricorn

Great Victoria Desert

Lake Eyre

Norfolk Island

Nullarbor Plain

Lake Torrens

FLINDERS RANGE

Darling

Murrumbidgee

Lord Howe Island

Great

Murray

AUSTRALIAN ALPS ▲2230 Mt. Kosciusko

Tasman Sea

North Island

Bass Strait

Tasmania

Cook Strait

South Island

▲3764 Mt. Cook

SOUTHERN OCEAN

Stewart Island

40°S

Modified Zenithal Equidistant Projection
© Oxford University Press

120°E

140°E

160°E

180°

40°S

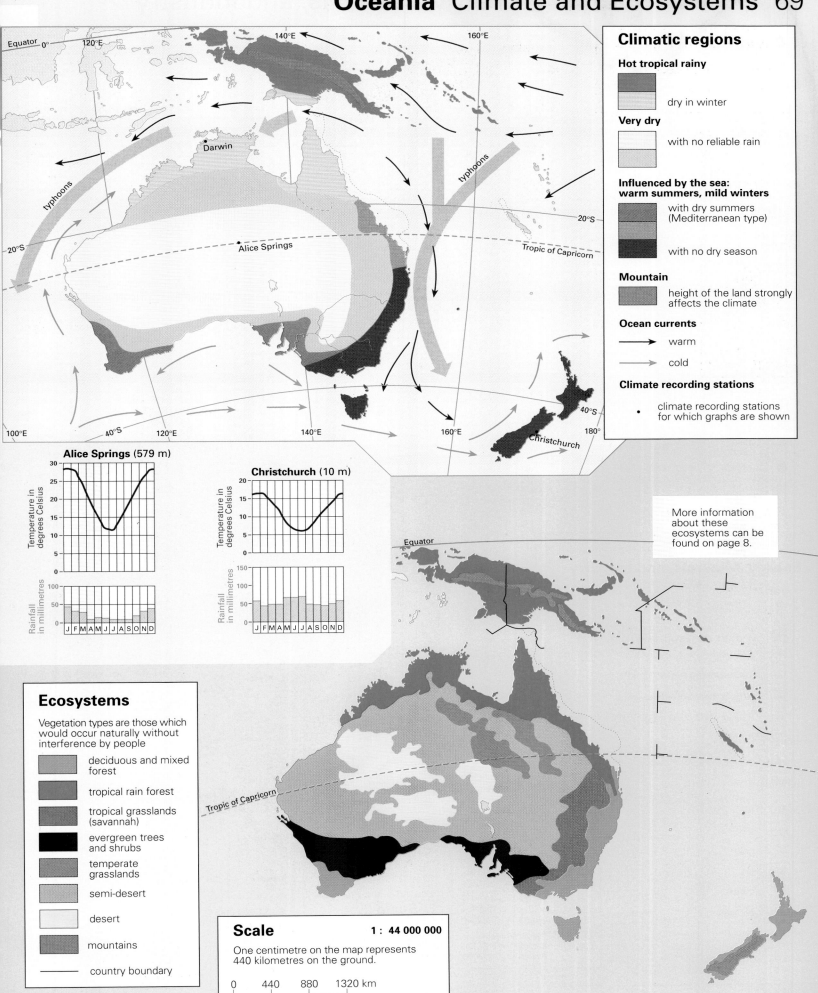

Climatic regions

Hot tropical rainy

dry in winter

Very dry

with no reliable rain

Influenced by the sea: warm summers, mild winters

with dry summers (Mediterranean type)

with no dry season

Mountain

height of the land strongly affects the climate

Ocean currents

→ warm

→ cold

Climate recording stations

• climate recording stations for which graphs are shown

Equator 0° 120°E 140°E 160°E

Darwin

20°S

Alice Springs

Tropic of Capricorn

typhoons

typhoons

20°S

100°E 40°S 120°E 140°E 160°E 180°

40°S

Christchurch

Alice Springs (579 m)

Temperature in degrees Celsius

Rainfall in millimetres

J F M A M J J A S O N D

Christchurch (10 m)

Temperature in degrees Celsius

Rainfall in millimetres

J F M A M J J A S O N D

More information about these ecosystems can be found on page 8.

Equator

Tropic of Capricorn

Ecosystems

Vegetation types are those which would occur naturally without interference by people

deciduous and mixed forest

tropical rain forest

tropical grasslands (savannah)

evergreen trees and shrubs

temperate grasslands

semi-desert

desert

mountains

—— country boundary

Scale

1 : 44 000 000

One centimetre on the map represents 440 kilometres on the ground.

0 440 880 1320 km

Oceania Farming, Energy, Minerals, and Industry

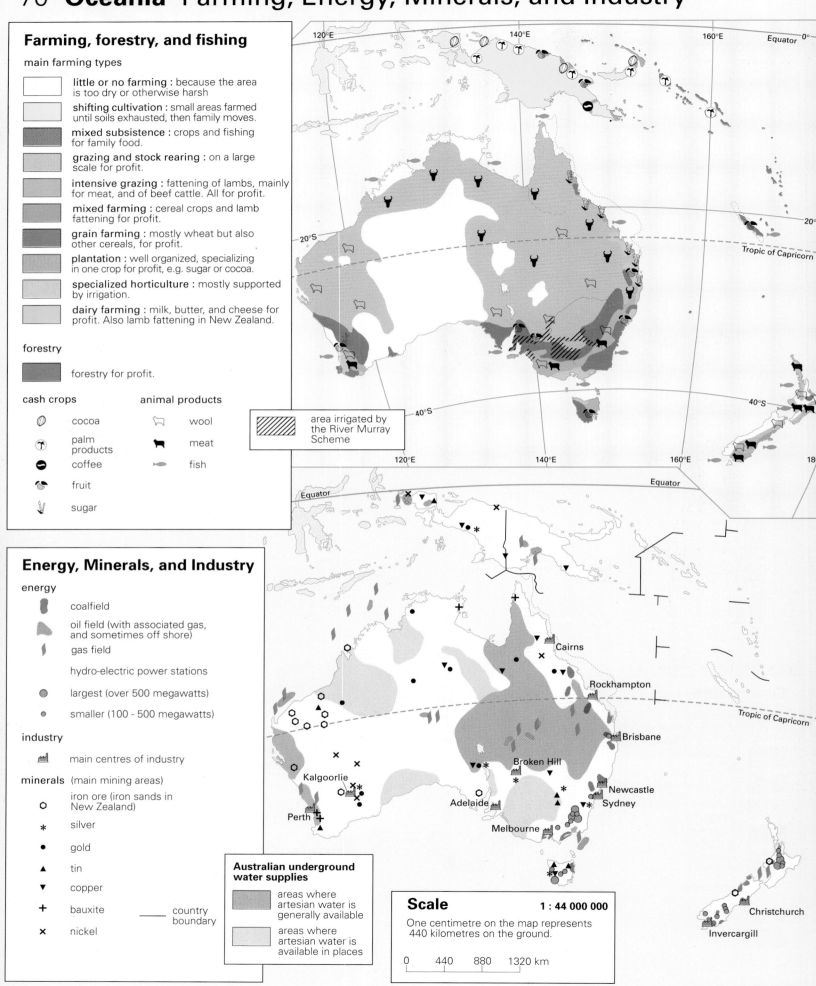

Farming, forestry, and fishing

main farming types

- **little or no farming :** because the area is too dry or otherwise harsh
- **shifting cultivation :** small areas farmed until soils exhausted, then family moves.
- **mixed subsistence :** crops and fishing for family food.
- **grazing and stock rearing :** on a large scale for profit.
- **intensive grazing :** fattening of lambs, mainly for meat, and of beef cattle. All for profit.
- **mixed farming :** cereal crops and lamb fattening for profit.
- **grain farming :** mostly wheat but also other cereals, for profit.
- **plantation :** well organized, specializing in one crop for profit, e.g. sugar or cocoa.
- **specialized horticulture :** mostly supported by irrigation.
- **dairy farming :** milk, butter, and cheese for profit. Also lamb fattening in New Zealand.

forestry

- forestry for profit.

cash crops

- cocoa
- palm products
- coffee
- fruit
- sugar

animal products

- wool
- meat
- fish

area irrigated by the River Murray Scheme

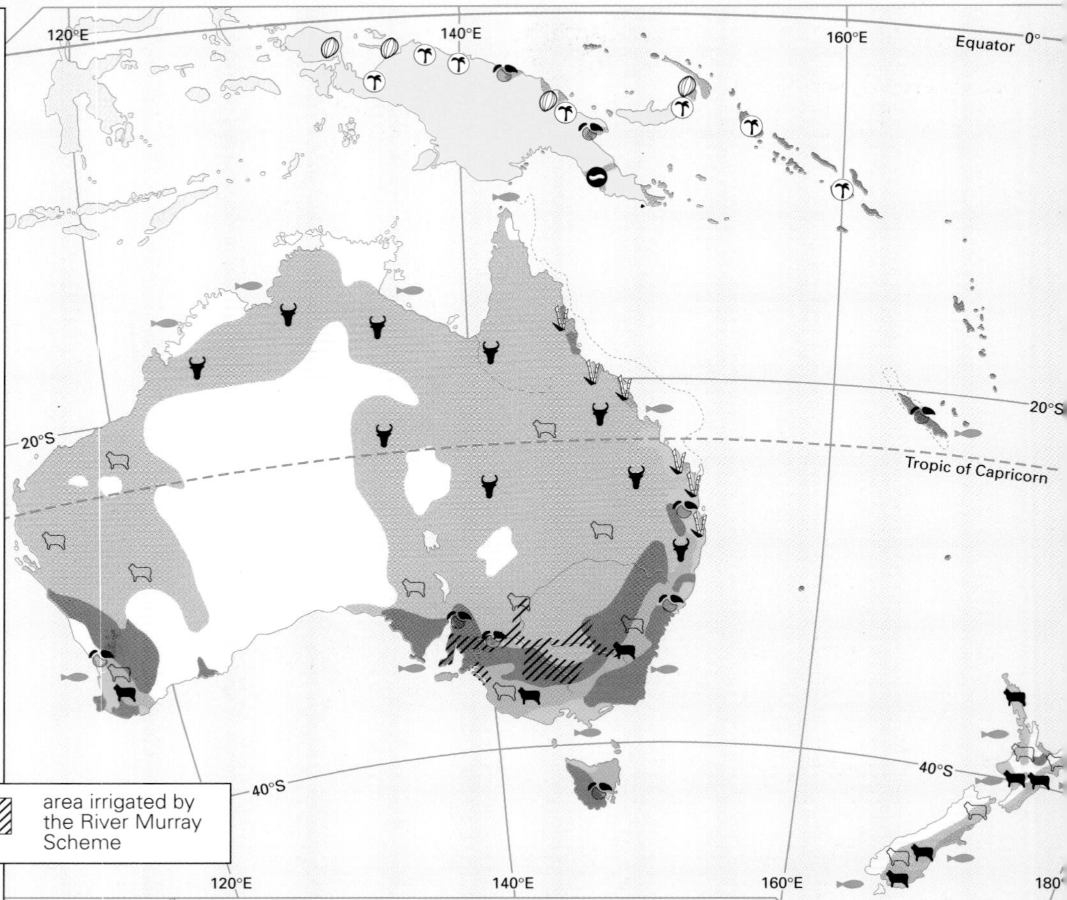
120°E
140°E
160°E
Equator
0°
20°S
20°S
Tropic of Capricorn
40°S
40°S
120°E
140°E
160°E
180°

Energy, Minerals, and Industry

energy

- coalfield
- oil field (with associated gas, and sometimes off shore)
- gas field

hydro-electric power stations

- largest (over 500 megawatts)
- smaller (100 - 500 megawatts)

industry

- main centres of industry

minerals (main mining areas)

- iron ore (iron sands in New Zealand)
- silver
- gold
- tin
- copper
- bauxite
- nickel

country boundary

Australian underground water supplies

- areas where artesian water is generally available
- areas where artesian water is available in places

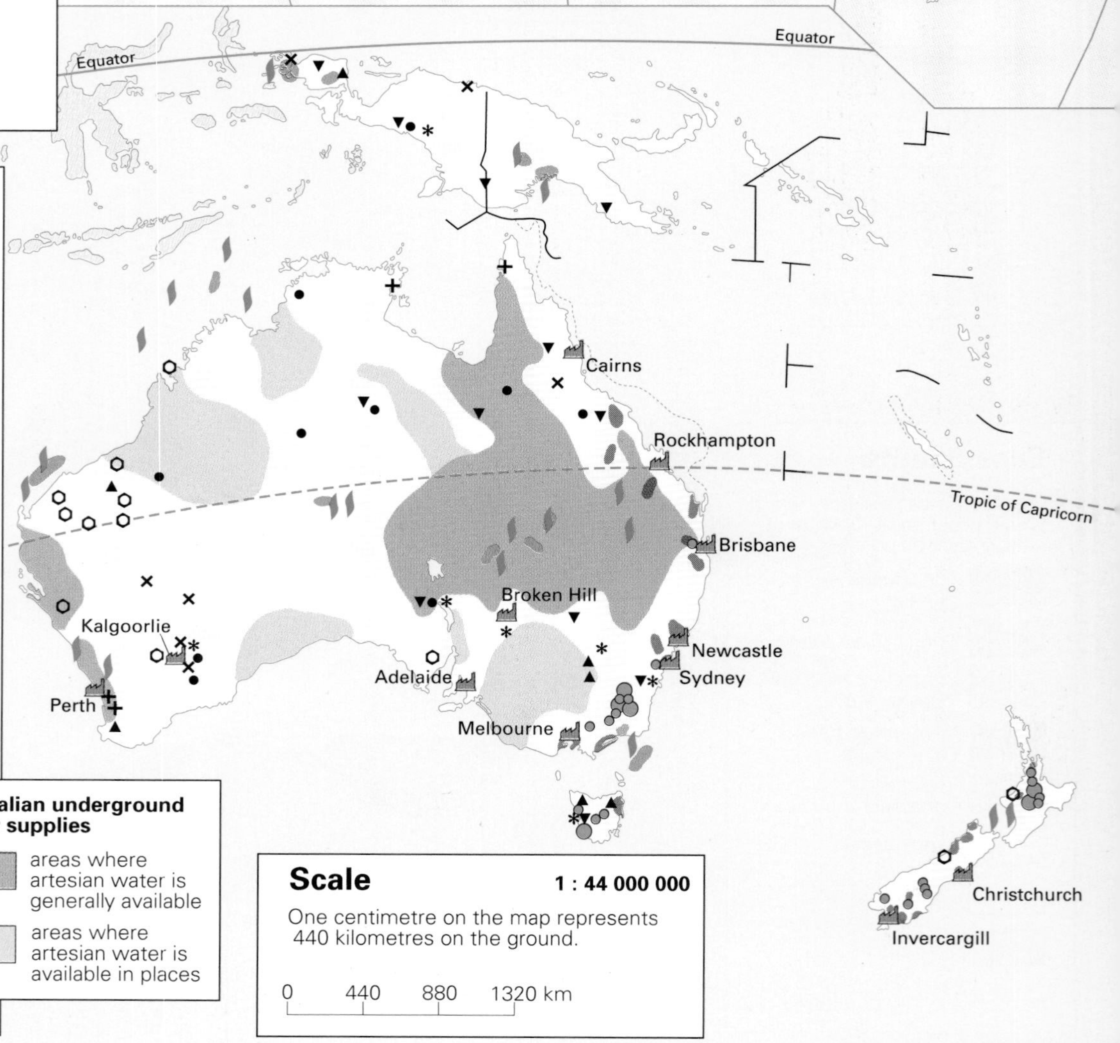
Equator
Equator
Cairns
Rockhampton
Tropic of Capricorn
Brisbane
Broken Hill
Kalgoorlie
Newcastle
Sydney
Adelaide
Perth
Melbourne
Christchurch
Invercargill

Scale **1 : 44 000 000**

One centimetre on the map represents 440 kilometres on the ground.

0 440 880 1320 km

Modified Zenithal Equidistant Projection

© Oxford University Press

Half of Australia's population live in the four cities of Sydney, Melbourne, Adelaide, and Perth.

Population density

number of people
per square kilometre

moderate		10-100
sparse		1-10
very low		less than 1

○ major cities and built up areas of at least 3 million people

• cities with 1 - 3 million people

── country boundary

Equator

Tropic of Capricorn

opic of Capricorn

Perth

Adelaide

Sydney

Melbourne

Population structure of New Zealand

Age

Males   Females

80
70
60
50
40
30
20
10
0

5 4 3 2 1 0   0 1 2 3 4 5

percent of population in 1992

Total population : 3.4 million

Population structure of Australia

Age

Males   Females

80
70
60
50
40
30
20
10

5 4 3 2 1 0   0 1 2 3 4 5

percent of population in 1994

Total population : 17.8 million

Scale   1 : 44 000 000

One centimetre on the map represents 440 kilometres on the ground.

0   440   880   1320 km

140°E

120°E

Equator   0°

Equator   0°

160°E

New Guinea

Queensland

20°S

Tropic of Capricorn

20°S

Great Australian Desert

Sydney

Melbourne

Auckland

40°S

40°S

Christchurch

180°

Environmental issues

tropical deforestation

existing areas of rainforest

former areas of rainforest

desertification

high risk areas

moderate risk areas

sea pollution

areas severely polluted for all or part of the year

areas persistently affected by pollution

▼ deep sea dump sites

air pollution

◇ cities where sulphur dioxide emmissions are recorded, and exceed recommended levels

bushfires

area at risk from bushfires for at least 4 months each year

global warming

addition of greenhouse gases in tonnes of carbon per person
(look at the world map on page 17)

Modified Zenithal Equidistant Projection
© Oxford University Press

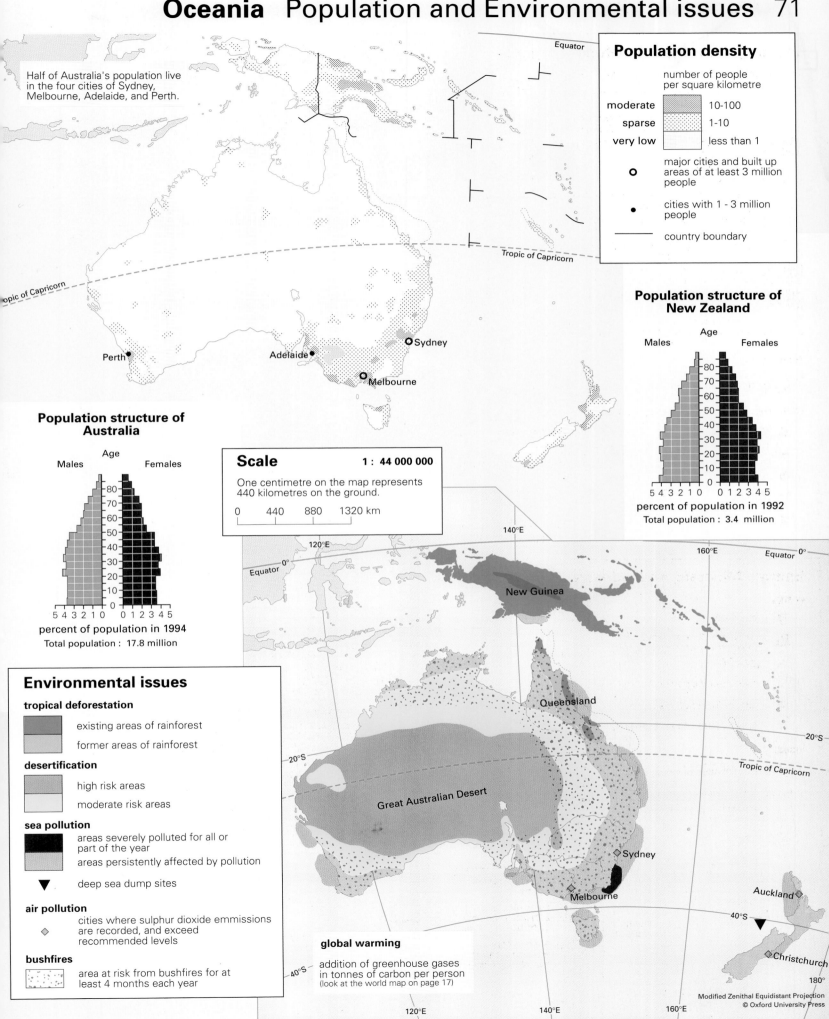

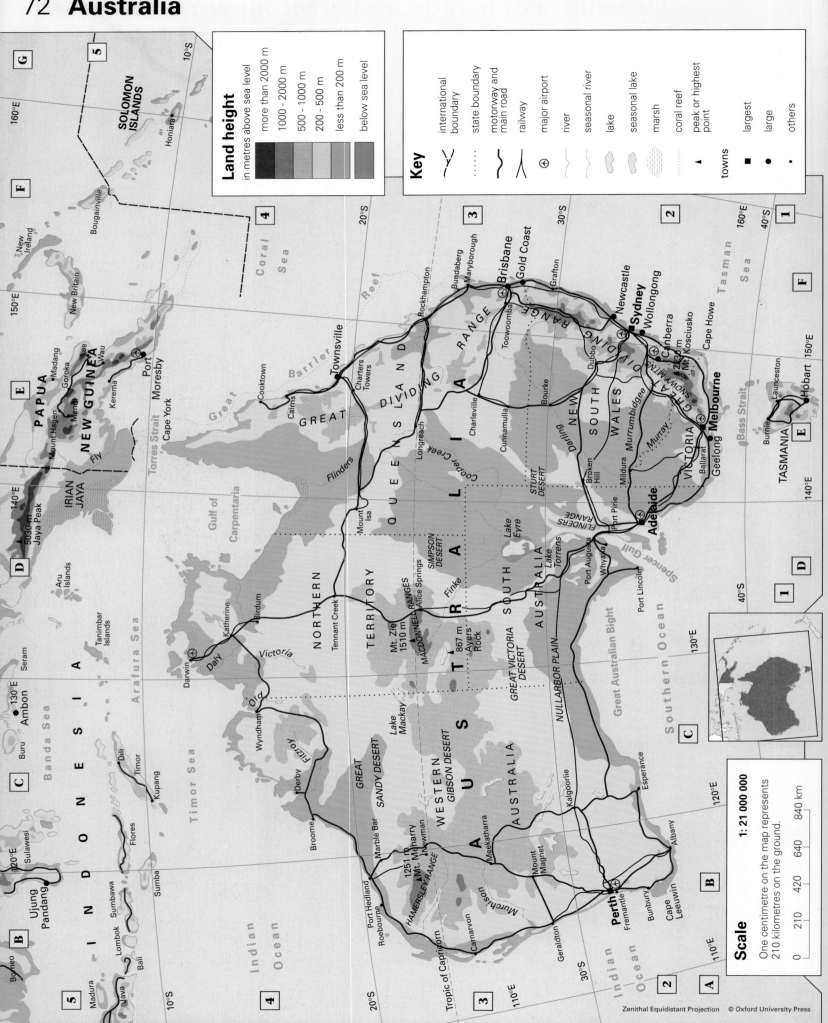

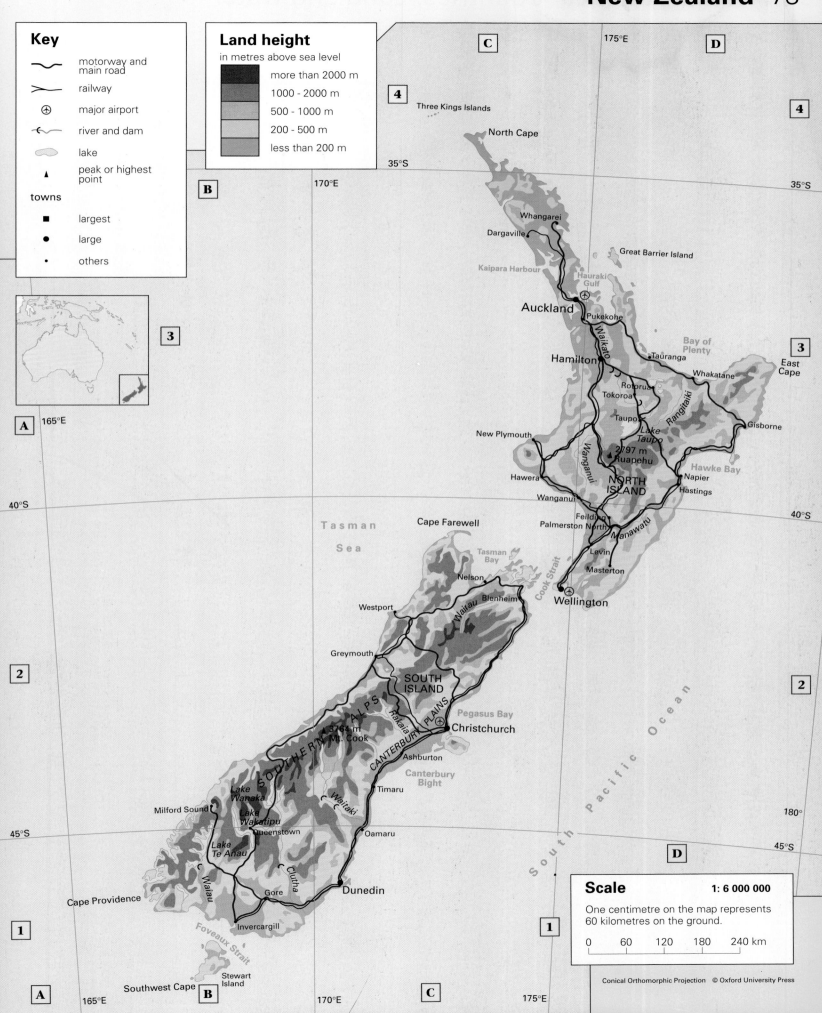

Key

motorway and main road	
railway	
major airport	⊕
river and dam	
lake	
peak or highest point	▲

towns

■	largest
●	large
·	others

Land height
in metres above sea level

- more than 2000 m
- 1000 - 2000 m
- 500 - 1000 m
- 200 - 500 m
- less than 200 m

Three Kings Islands

North Cape

Whangarei

Dargaville

Kaipara Harbour

Great Barrier Island

Hauraki Gulf

Auckland

Pukekohe

Waikato

Bay of Plenty

Hamilton

Tauranga

Rotorua

Whakatane

Tokoroa

East Cape

Taupo

Rangitaiki

New Plymouth

Lake Taupo

Gisborne

▲2797 m Ruapehu

Wanganui

Hawke Bay

Hawera

NORTH ISLAND

Napier

Hastings

Wanganui

Feilding

Palmerston North

Manawatu

Cape Farewell

Tasman Sea

Levin

Masterton

Tasman Bay

Nelson

Cook Strait

Wellington

Westport

Wairau

Blenheim

Greymouth

SOUTH ISLAND

Pegasus Bay

▲3764 m Mt. Cook

SOUTHERN ALPS

Rakaia

CANTERBURY PLAINS

Christchurch

Ashburton

Canterbury Bight

Lake Wanaka

Waitaki

Timaru

Milford Sound

Lake Wakatipu

Queenstown

Oamaru

Lake Te Anau

Clutha

Waiau

Gore

Dunedin

Cape Providence

Invercargill

Foveaux Strait

Stewart Island

Southwest Cape

South Pacific Ocean

Scale
1: 6 000 000

One centimetre on the map represents 60 kilometres on the ground.

0	60	120	180	240 km

Conical Orthomorphic Projection   © Oxford University Press

165°E · 170°E · 175°E · 180°
35°S · 40°S · 45°S

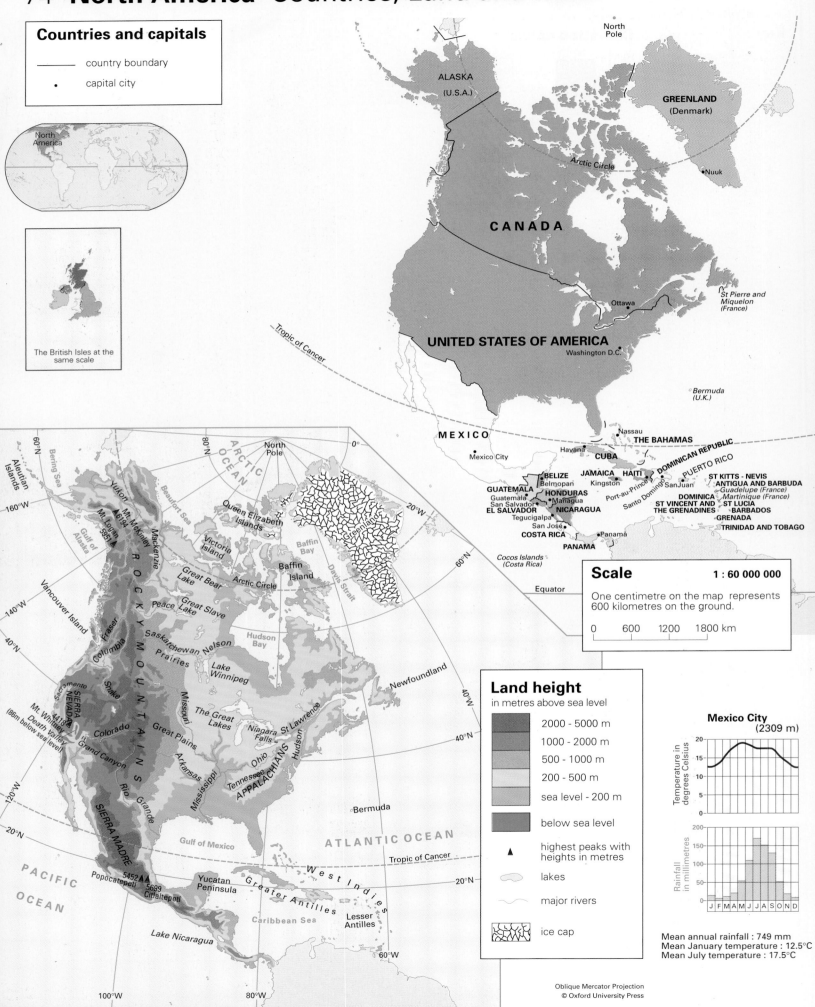

Countries and capitals

— country boundary

• capital city

North America

The British Isles at the same scale

Scale 1 : 60 000 000

One centimetre on the map represents 600 kilometres on the ground.

0 600 1200 1800 km

Land height
in metres above sea level

- 2000 - 5000 m
- 1000 - 2000 m
- 500 - 1000 m
- 200 - 500 m
- sea level - 200 m
- below sea level

▲ highest peaks with heights in metres

lakes

major rivers

ice cap

Mexico City
(2309 m)

Temperature in degrees Celsius

Rainfall in millimetres

J F M A M J J A S O N D

Mean annual rainfall : 749 mm
Mean January temperature : 12.5°C
Mean July temperature : 17.5°C

Oblique Mercator Projection
© Oxford University Press

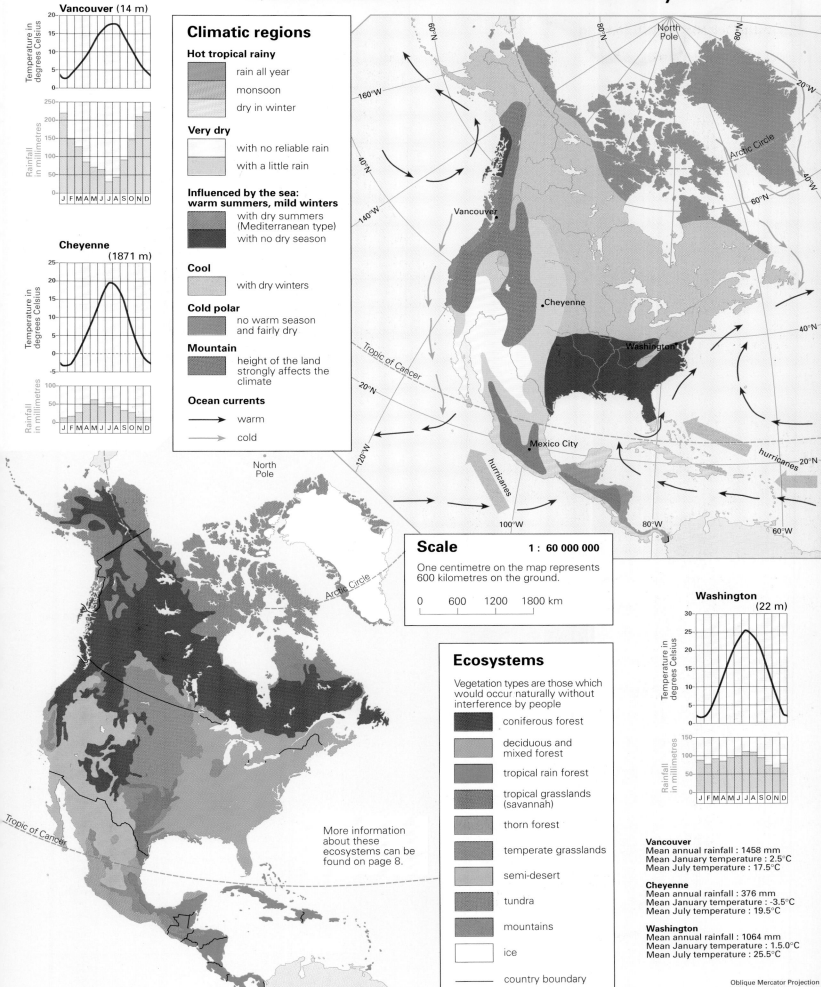

Vancouver (14 m)
Temperature in degrees Celsius
Rainfall in millimetres
J F M A M J J A S O N D

Cheyenne (1871 m)
Temperature in degrees Celsius
Rainfall in millimetres
J F M A M J J A S O N D

Climatic regions

Hot tropical rainy
- rain all year
- monsoon
- dry in winter

Very dry
- with no reliable rain
- with a little rain

Influenced by the sea: warm summers, mild winters
- with dry summers (Mediterranean type)
- with no dry season

Cool
- with dry winters

Cold polar
- no warm season and fairly dry

Mountain
- height of the land strongly affects the climate

Ocean currents
- → warm
- → cold

Scale   1 : 60 000 000
One centimetre on the map represents 600 kilometres on the ground.

0   600   1200   1800 km

Ecosystems

Vegetation types are those which would occur naturally without interference by people

- coniferous forest
- deciduous and mixed forest
- tropical rain forest
- tropical grasslands (savannah)
- thorn forest
- temperate grasslands
- semi-desert
- tundra
- mountains
- ice
- —— country boundary

More information about these ecosystems can be found on page 8.

Washington (22 m)
Temperature in degrees Celsius
Rainfall in millimetres
J F M A M J J A S O N D

Vancouver
Mean annual rainfall : 1458 mm
Mean January temperature : 2.5°C
Mean July temperature : 17.5°C

Cheyenne
Mean annual rainfall : 376 mm
Mean January temperature : -3.5°C
Mean July temperature : 19.5°C

Washington
Mean annual rainfall : 1064 mm
Mean January temperature : 1.5.0°C
Mean July temperature : 25.5°C

Oblique Mercator Projection
© Oxford University Press

Farming, forestry, and fishing

main farming types

little or no farming : because the area is too cold or otherwise harsh

trapping and fishing : for family food. Furs and surplus fish sold for profit.

shifting cultivation : small areas farmed until soils exhausted, then family moves.

mixed subsistence : crops and animals for family food.

subsistance crops : mostly intensive with the aid of irrigation. Family food only.

grazing and stock rearing : on a large scale, for profit.

mixed farming : animals and crops for profit.

grain farming : mostly wheat, on a large scale, for profit.

plantation : well organized, specializing in one crop for profit, e.g. cotton.

mediterranean farming : cereals, animals, vegetables, fruit, wine, surplus for profit.

specialized horticulture : often supported by irrigation.

dairy farming : milk, butter, and cheese for profit.

forestry cutting and replacement of timber for profit

cash crops

- cocoa
- groundnuts
- coffee
- cotton
- tobacco
- fruit
- sugar

animal products

- meat
- fish

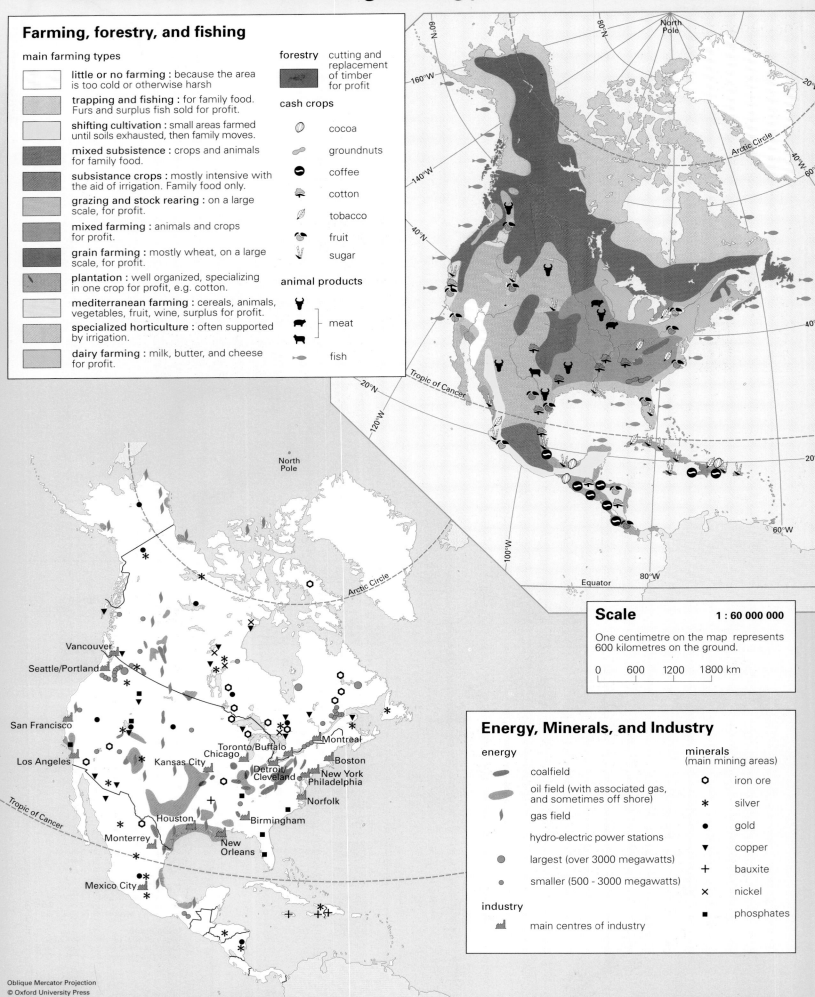

Scale 1 : 60 000 000

One centimetre on the map represents 600 kilometres on the ground.

0   600   1200   1800 km

Energy, Minerals, and Industry

energy

- coalfield
- oil field (with associated gas, and sometimes off shore)
- gas field
- hydro-electric power stations
- largest (over 3000 megawatts)
- smaller (500 - 3000 megawatts)

industry

- main centres of industry

minerals
(main mining areas)

- iron ore
- silver
- gold
- copper
- bauxite
- nickel
- phosphates

Oblique Mercator Projection
© Oxford University Press

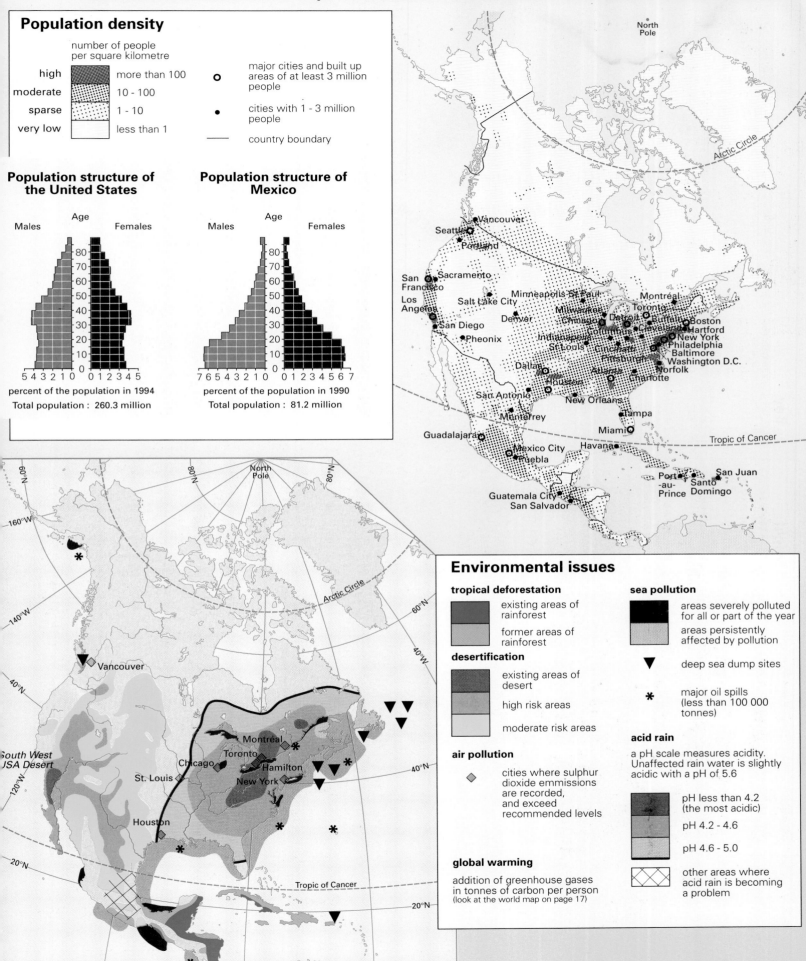

Population density

number of people
per square kilometre

high	more than 100
moderate	10 - 100
sparse	1 - 10
very low	less than 1

○ major cities and built up areas of at least 3 million people

• cities with 1 - 3 million people

— country boundary

Population structure of the United States

Age

Males — Females

percent of the population in 1994
Total population : 260.3 million

Population structure of Mexico

Age

Males — Females

percent of the population in 1990
Total population : 81.2 million

Environmental issues

tropical deforestation
- existing areas of rainforest
- former areas of rainforest

desertification
- existing areas of desert
- high risk areas
- moderate risk areas

air pollution
- ◆ cities where sulphur dioxide emmissions are recorded, and exceed recommended levels

global warming
addition of greenhouse gases in tonnes of carbon per person
(look at the world map on page 17)

sea pollution
- areas severely polluted for all or part of the year
- areas persistently affected by pollution
- ▼ deep sea dump sites
- ✳ major oil spills (less than 100 000 tonnes)

acid rain
a pH scale measures acidity. Unaffected rain water is slightly acidic with a pH of 5.6
- pH less than 4.2 (the most acidic)
- pH 4.2 - 4.6
- pH 4.6 - 5.0
- other areas where acid rain is becoming a problem

Oblique Mercator Projection
© Oxford University Press

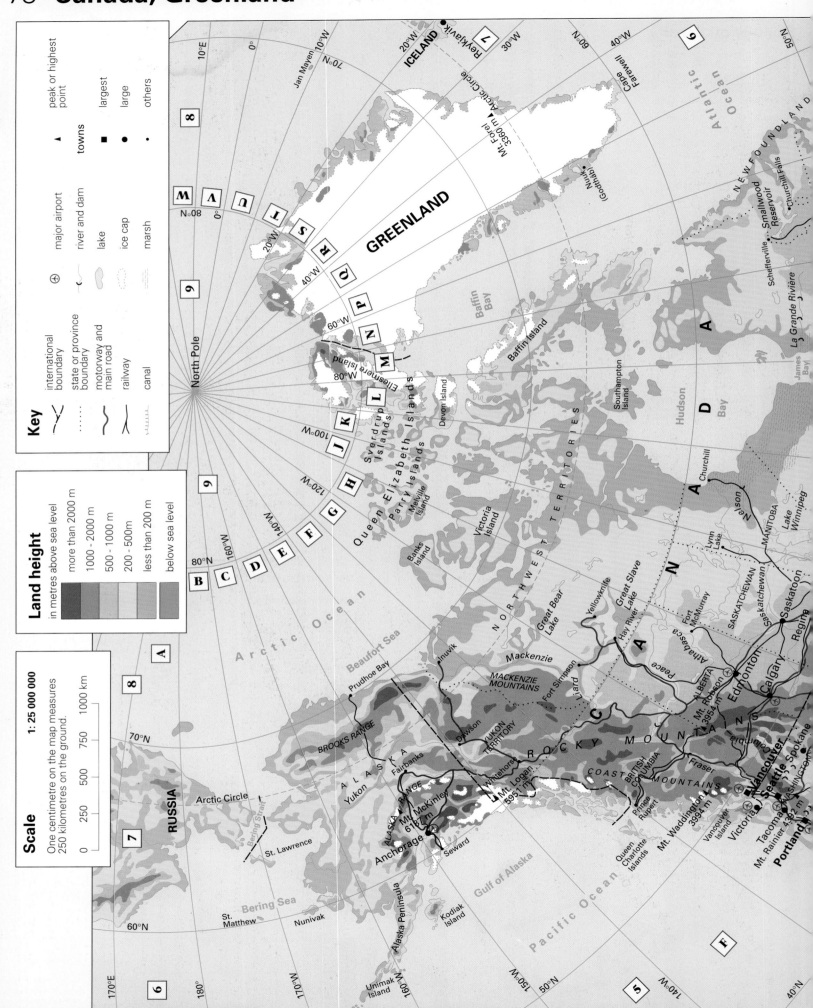

Key

	international boundary	
	state or province boundary	
	motorway and main road	
	railway	
	canal	

	peak or highest point	
towns		
■	largest	
●	large	
·	others	

⊕	major airport
	river and dam
	lake
	ice cap
	marsh

Land height

in metres above sea level

	more than 2000 m
	1000 - 2000 m
	500 - 1000 m
	200 - 500m
	less than 200 m
	below sea level

Scale   1: 25 000 000

One centimetre on the map measures
250 kilometres on the ground.

0 250 500 750 1000 km

GREENLAND

ICELAND

Reykjavik

Mt. Forel
3360 m

Nuuk
(Godthåb)

Baffin
Bay

Baffin Island

Devon Island

Ellesmere Island

Sverdrup
Islands

Queen Elizabeth Islands

Parry Islands

Melville
Island

Victoria
Island

Banks
Island

Southampton
Island

Hudson
Bay

NEWFOUNDLAND

Smallwood
Reservoir

Schefferville

Churchill Falls

La Grande Rivière

James
Bay

Atlantic
Ocean

Cape
Farewell

North Pole

Arctic Ocean

Beaufort Sea

Prudhoe Bay

Inuvik

Mackenzie

Fort Simpson

MACKENZIE
MOUNTAINS

Great Bear
Lake

Great Slave
Lake

Hay River

Yellowknife

Liard

Peace

Fort
McMurray

Athabasca

NORTHWEST TERRITORIES

Churchill

Nelson

Lynn
Lake

MANITOBA

Lake
Winnipeg

SASKATCHEWAN

Saskatoon

Saskatchewan

Regina

ALBERTA

Mt. Robson
3954 m

Edmonton

Calgary

C A N A D A

BROOKS RANGE

Fairbanks

Yukon

ALASKA

Dawson

YUKON
TERRITORY

Whitehorse

Mt. Logan
5951 m

Mt. McKinley
6187 m

Anchorage

Seward

ALASKA RANGE

R O C K Y   M O U N T A I N S

BRITISH
COLUMBIA

COAST

MOUNTAINS

Columbia

Fraser

Prince
Rupert

Queen
Charlotte
Islands

Mt. Waddington
3994 m

Vancouver
Island

Victoria

Vancouver

Seattle

Tacoma

WASHINGTON

Spokane

Mt. Rainier 4392 m

Portland

Gulf of Alaska

Pacific
Ocean

RUSSIA

Bering Strait

St. Lawrence

St. Matthew

Nunivak

Bering Sea

Unimak
Island

Alaska Peninsula

Kodiak
Island

Arctic Circle

Jan Mayen

A B C D E F G H J K L M N O P Q R S T U V W

5 6 7 8 9

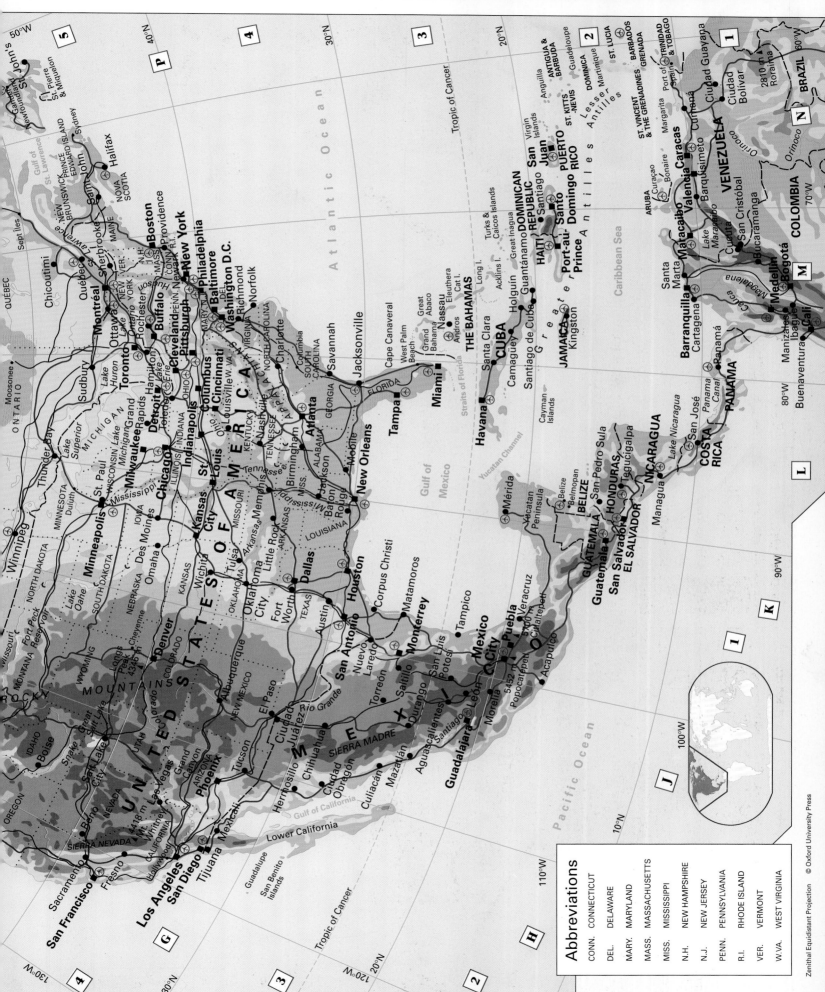

Abbreviations

CONN.	CONNECTICUT
DEL.	DELAWARE
MARY.	MARYLAND
MASS.	MASSACHUSETTS
MISS.	MISSISSIPPI
N.H.	NEW HAMPSHIRE
N.J.	NEW JERSEY
PENN.	PENNSYLVANIA
R.I.	RHODE ISLAND
VER.	VERMONT
W.VA.	WEST VIRGINIA

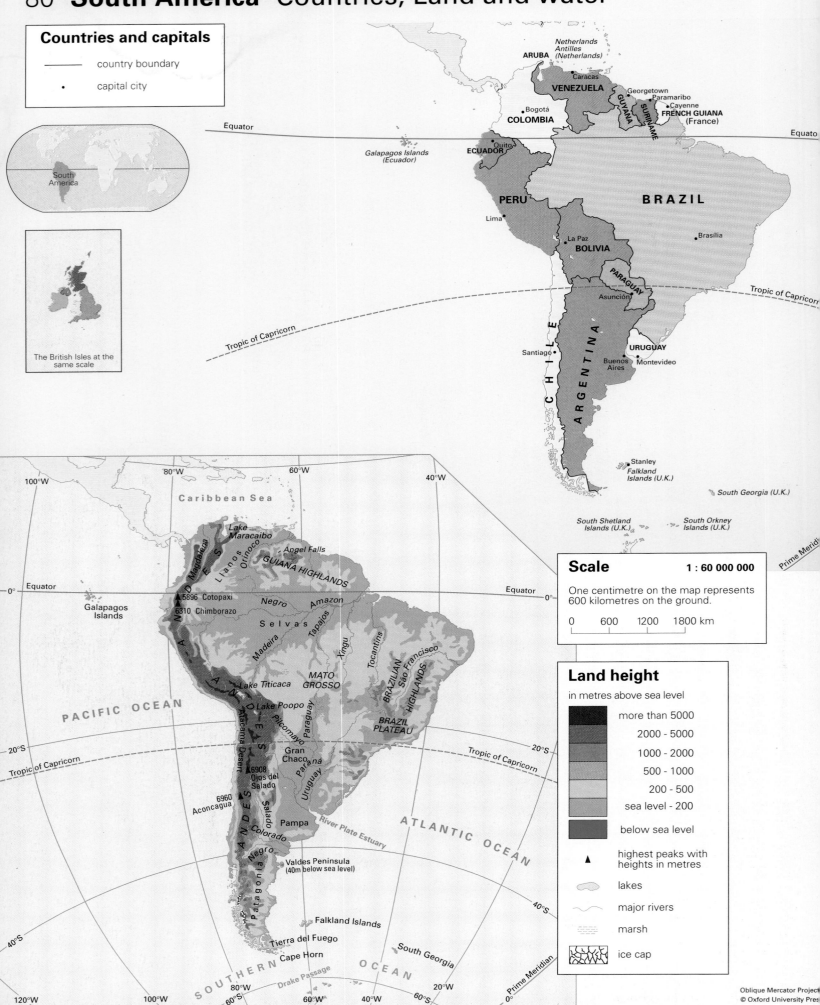

Countries and capitals

— country boundary

• capital city

South America

The British Isles at the same scale

ARUBA
Netherlands Antilles (Netherlands)
Caracas
VENEZUELA
Georgetown
Paramaribo
GUYANA
SURINAME
Cayenne
FRENCH GUIANA (France)
• Bogotá
COLOMBIA
Equator   Equator
Quito•
ECUADOR
Galapagos Islands (Ecuador)
PERU   BRAZIL
Lima•
• La Paz   • Brasília
BOLIVIA
PARAGUAY
Tropic of Capricorn   Tropic of Capricorn
Asunción•
C
H
I
L
E
A
R
G
E
N
T
I
N
A
URUGUAY
Santiago•
Buenos Aires• • Montevideo

• Stanley
Falkland Islands (U.K.)
South Georgia (U.K.)
South Shetland Islands (U.K.)
South Orkney Islands (U.K.)

Scale   1 : 60 000 000

One centimetre on the map represents 600 kilometres on the ground.

0   600   1200   1800 km

Caribbean Sea
Lake Maracaibo
Orinoco
Llanos
Angel Falls
GUIANA HIGHLANDS
A
N
D
E
S
Magdalena
▲5896 Cotopaxi
6310 Chimborazo
Negro
Amazon
S e l v a s
Tapajos
Madeira
Xingu
Tocantins
São Francisco
BRAZILIAN HIGHLANDS
Lake Titicaca
MATO GROSSO
Lake Poopo
Pilcomayo
Paraguay
Paraná
Uruguay
BRAZIL PLATEAU
Galapagos Islands
Equator   Equator
PACIFIC OCEAN
Atacama Desert
A
N
D
E
S
▲6908 Ojos del Salado
6960 ▲ Aconcagua
Salado
Colorado
Gran Chaco
Pampa
ATLANTIC OCEAN
River Plate Estuary
Tropic of Capricorn   Tropic of Capricorn
Negro
Patagonia
Valdes Peninsula (40m below sea level)
Falkland Islands
South Georgia
Tierra del Fuego
Cape Horn
SOUTHERN OCEAN
Drake Passage

Land height

in metres above sea level

more than 5000

2000 - 5000

1000 - 2000

500 - 1000

200 - 500

sea level - 200

below sea level

▲ highest peaks with heights in metres

lakes

major rivers

marsh

ice cap

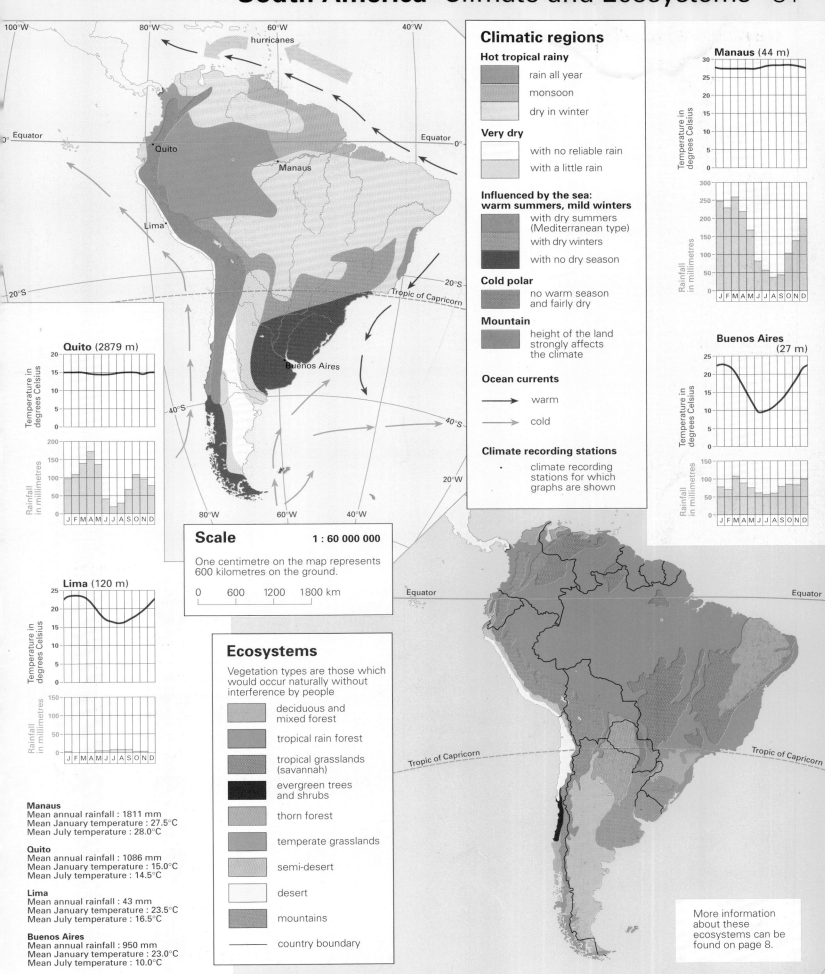

Climatic regions

Hot tropical rainy
- rain all year
- monsoon
- dry in winter

Very dry
- with no reliable rain
- with a little rain

Influenced by the sea: warm summers, mild winters
- with dry summers (Mediterranean type)
- with dry winters
- with no dry season

Cold polar
- no warm season and fairly dry

Mountain
- height of the land strongly affects the climate

Ocean currents
- → warm
- → cold

Climate recording stations
- · climate recording stations for which graphs are shown

Manaus (44 m)

Buenos Aires (27 m)

Quito (2879 m)

Lima (120 m)

Scale 1 : 60 000 000

One centimetre on the map represents 600 kilometres on the ground.

0   600   1200   1800 km

Ecosystems

Vegetation types are those which would occur naturally without interference by people

- deciduous and mixed forest
- tropical rain forest
- tropical grasslands (savannah)
- evergreen trees and shrubs
- thorn forest
- temperate grasslands
- semi-desert
- desert
- mountains
- —— country boundary

Manaus
Mean annual rainfall : 1811 mm
Mean January temperature : 27.5°C
Mean July temperature : 28.0°C

Quito
Mean annual rainfall : 1086 mm
Mean January temperature : 15.0°C
Mean July temperature : 14.5°C

Lima
Mean annual rainfall : 43 mm
Mean January temperature : 23.5°C
Mean July temperature : 16.5°C

Buenos Aires
Mean annual rainfall : 950 mm
Mean January temperature : 23.0°C
Mean July temperature : 10.0°C

More information about these ecosystems can be found on page 8.

hurricanes

Equator

Quito

Manaus

Lima

Tropic of Capricorn

Buenos Aires

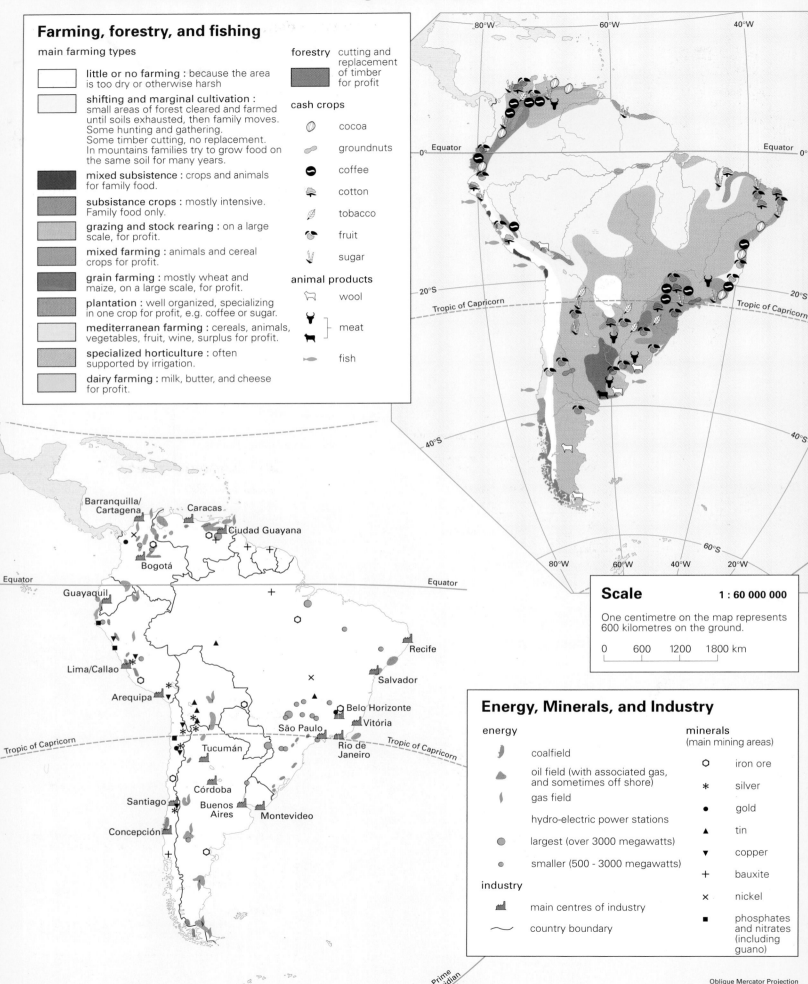

Farming, forestry, and fishing

main farming types

little or no farming : because the area is too dry or otherwise harsh

shifting and marginal cultivation : small areas of forest cleared and farmed until soils exhausted, then family moves. Some hunting and gathering. Some timber cutting, no replacement. In mountains families try to grow food on the same soil for many years.

mixed subsistence : crops and animals for family food.

subsistance crops : mostly intensive. Family food only.

grazing and stock rearing : on a large scale, for profit.

mixed farming : animals and cereal crops for profit.

grain farming : mostly wheat and maize, on a large scale, for profit.

plantation : well organized, specializing in one crop for profit, e.g. coffee or sugar.

mediterranean farming : cereals, animals, vegetables, fruit, wine, surplus for profit.

specialized horticulture : often supported by irrigation.

dairy farming : milk, butter, and cheese for profit.

forestry cutting and replacement of timber for profit

cash crops

- cocoa
- groundnuts
- coffee
- cotton
- tobacco
- fruit
- sugar

animal products

- wool
- meat
- fish

Scale

1 : 60 000 000

One centimetre on the map represents 600 kilometres on the ground.

0   600   1200   1800 km

Energy, Minerals, and Industry

energy

- coalfield
- oil field (with associated gas, and sometimes off shore)
- gas field

hydro-electric power stations

- largest (over 3000 megawatts)
- smaller (500 - 3000 megawatts)

industry

- main centres of industry
- country boundary

minerals (main mining areas)

- ○ iron ore
- * silver
- • gold
- ▲ tin
- ▼ copper
- + bauxite
- × nickel
- ■ phosphates and nitrates (including guano)

Barranquilla/Cartagena
Caracas
Ciudad Guayana
Bogotá
Guayaquil
Lima/Callao
Arequipa
Tucumán
Santiago
Córdoba
Concepción
Buenos Aires
Montevideo
São Paulo
Rio de Janeiro
Belo Horizonte
Vitória
Salvador
Recife

Oblique Mercator Projection
© Oxford University Press

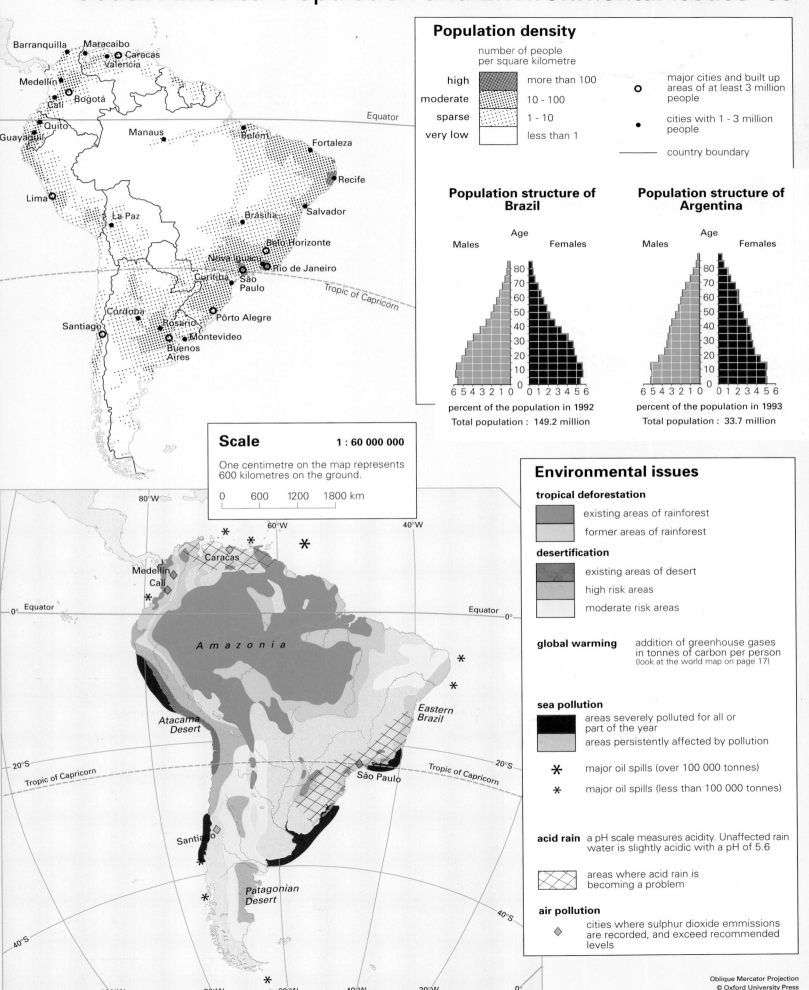

Population density

number of people per square kilometre

high		more than 100
moderate		10 - 100
sparse		1 - 10
very low		less than 1

○ major cities and built up areas of at least 3 million people

• cities with 1 - 3 million people

— country boundary

Population structure of Brazil

Age

Males — Females

percent of the population in 1992

Total population : 149.2 million

Population structure of Argentina

Age

Males — Females

percent of the population in 1993

Total population : 33.7 million

Scale

1 : 60 000 000

One centimetre on the map represents 600 kilometres on the ground.

0   600   1200   1800 km

Environmental issues

tropical deforestation

existing areas of rainforest

former areas of rainforest

desertification

existing areas of desert

high risk areas

moderate risk areas

global warming   addition of greenhouse gases in tonnes of carbon per person (look at the world map on page 17)

sea pollution

areas severely polluted for all or part of the year

areas persistently affected by pollution

✳ major oil spills (over 100 000 tonnes)

✳ major oil spills (less than 100 000 tonnes)

acid rain   a pH scale measures acidity. Unaffected rain water is slightly acidic with a pH of 5.6

areas where acid rain is becoming a problem

air pollution

cities where sulphur dioxide emmissions are recorded, and exceed recommended levels

Oblique Mercator Projection
© Oxford University Press

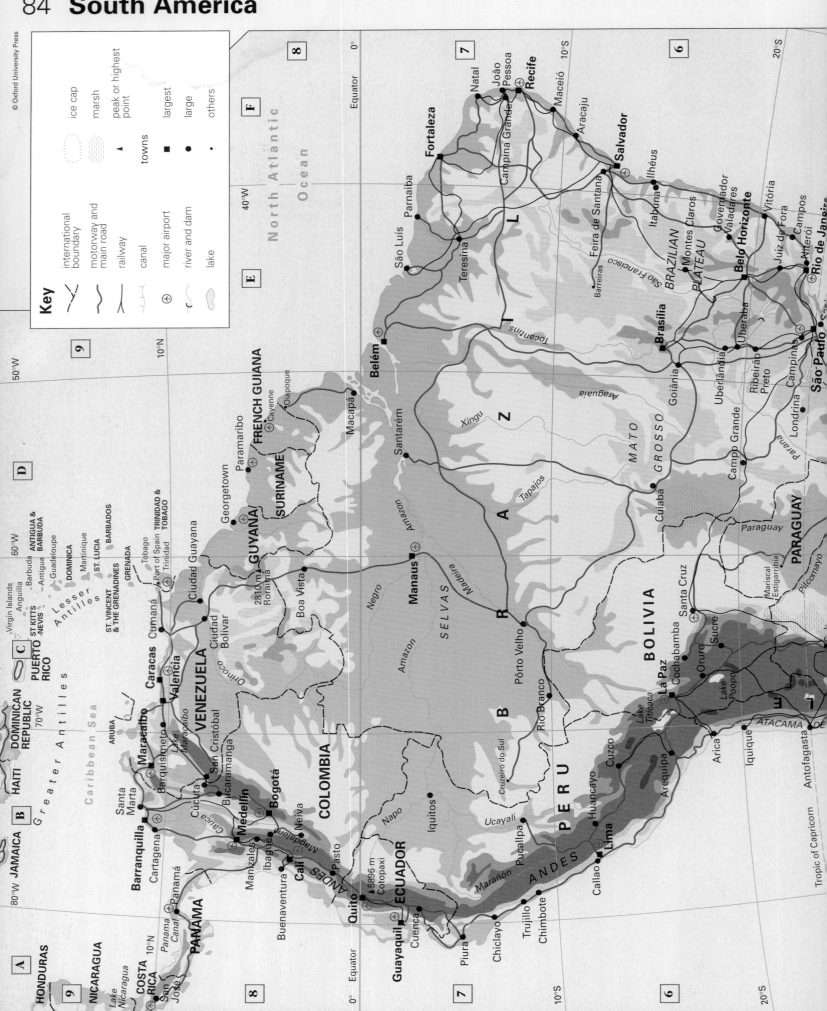

Key

international boundary	ice cap
motorway and main road	marsh
railway	peak or highest point
canal	
major airport	largest
river and dam	large
lake	others

towns

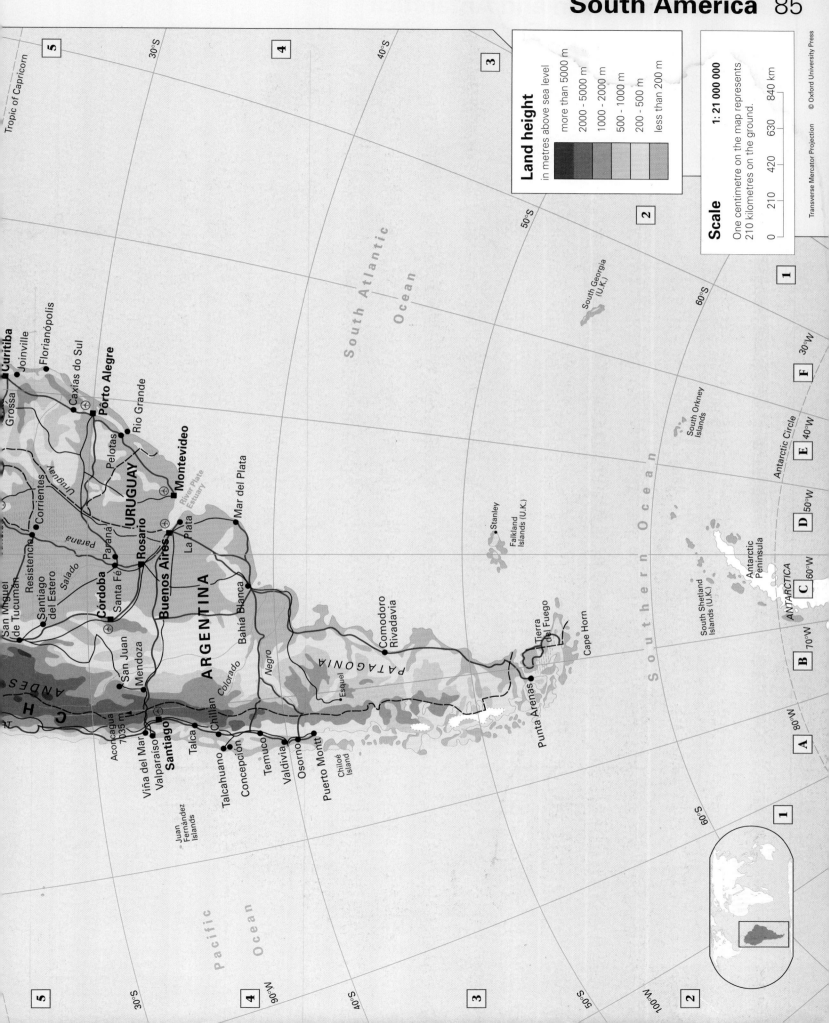

Land height
in metres above sea level

more than 5000 m
2000 - 5000 m
1000 - 2000 m
500 - 1000 m
200 - 500 m
less than 200 m

Scale   1: 21 000 000
One centimetre on the map represents
210 kilometres on the ground.

0   210   420   630   840 km

Transverse Mercator Projection   © Oxford University Press

Tropic of Capricorn

30°S

40°S

50°S

60°S

South Atlantic Ocean

South Georgia (U.K.)

South Orkney Islands

Antarctic Circle

South Shetland Islands (U.K.)

Antarctic Peninsula

ANTARCTICA

Southern Ocean

Stanley

Falkland Islands (U.K.)

Comodoro Rivadavia

PATAGONIA

Esquel

Punta Arenas

Tierra del Fuego

Cape Horn

Curitiba
Joinville
Florianópolis
Grossa
Caxias do Sul
Pôrto Alegre
Rio Grande
Pelotas
Montevideo
URUGUAY
Corrientes
Resistencia
Paraná
Uruguay
Salado
Parana
Santa Fé
Rosario
Córdoba
San Miguel de Tucumán
Santiago del Estero
San Juan
Mendoza
Acongagua 7035 m
Viña del Mar
Valparaíso
Santiago
Talca
Chillán
Talcahuano
Concepción
Temuco
Valdivia
Osorno
Puerto Montt
Chiloé Island
Juan Fernández Islands
CHILE
ANDES
ARGENTINA
Buenos Aires
La Plata
Mar del Plata
Bahía Blanca
Colorado
Negro
River Plate Estuary

Pacific Ocean

80°W
70°W
60°W
50°W
40°W
30°W

90°W
100°W

A B C D E F
1 2 3 4 5

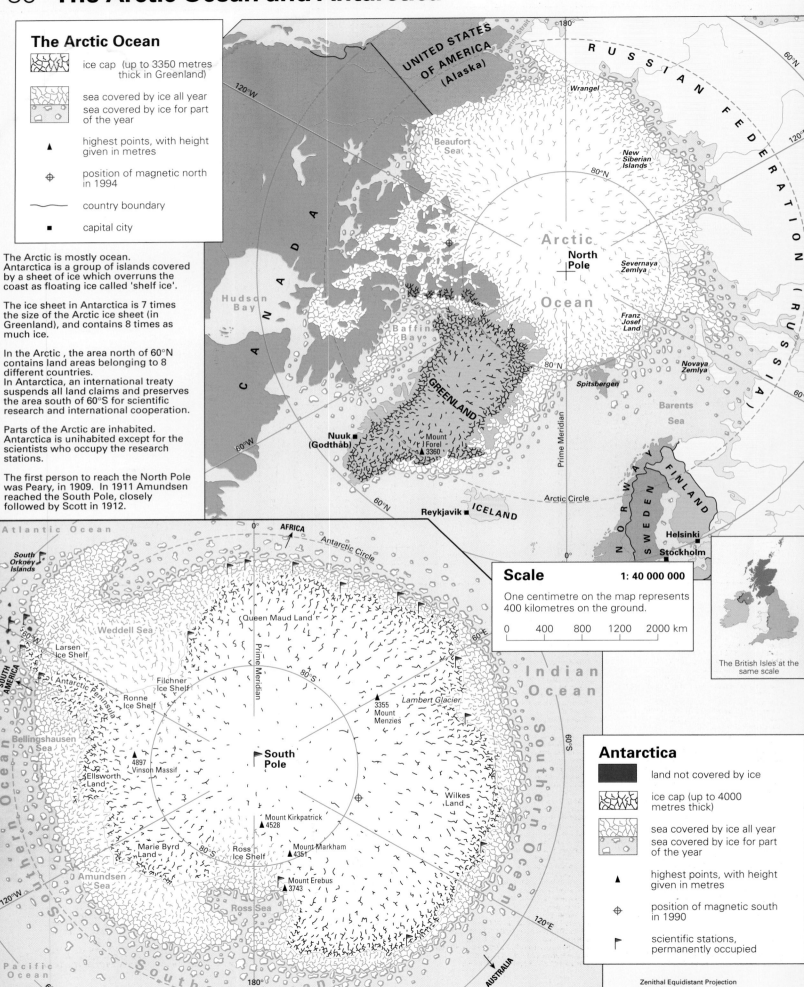

The Arctic Ocean

- ice cap (up to 3350 metres thick in Greenland)
- sea covered by ice all year
  sea covered by ice for part of the year
- ▲ highest points, with height given in metres
- ⊕ position of magnetic north in 1994
- country boundary
- ■ capital city

The Arctic is mostly ocean. Antarctica is a group of islands covered by a sheet of ice which overruns the coast as floating ice called 'shelf ice'.

The ice sheet in Antarctica is 7 times the size of the Arctic ice sheet (in Greenland), and contains 8 times as much ice.

In the Arctic , the area north of 60°N contains land areas belonging to 8 different countries.
In Antarctica, an international treaty suspends all land claims and preserves the area south of 60°S for scientific research and international cooperation.

Parts of the Arctic are inhabited. Antarctica is unihabited except for the scientists who occupy the research stations.

The first person to reach the North Pole was Peary, in 1909. In 1911 Amundsen reached the South Pole, closely followed by Scott in 1912.

Scale

1: 40 000 000

One centimetre on the map represents 400 kilometres on the ground.

0   400   800   1200   2000 km

The British Isles at the same scale

Antarctica

- land not covered by ice
- ice cap (up to 4000 metres thick)
- sea covered by ice all year
  sea covered by ice for part of the year
- ▲ highest points, with height given in metres
- ⊕ position of magnetic south in 1990
- ⚑ scientific stations, permanently occupied

Zenithal Equidistant Projection
© Oxford University Press

How to use the index

To find a place on an atlas map use either the grid code or latitude and longitude.

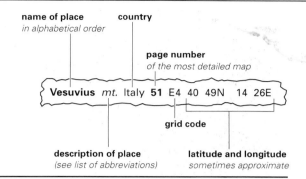

name of place
in alphabetical order

country

page number
of the most detailed map

Vesuvius *mt.* Italy **51** E4 40 49N 14 26E

grid code

description of place
(see list of abbreviations)

latitude and longitude
sometimes approximate

Grid code

Vesuvius is in grid square E4

Vesuvius *mt.* Italy **51** E4 40 49N 14 26E

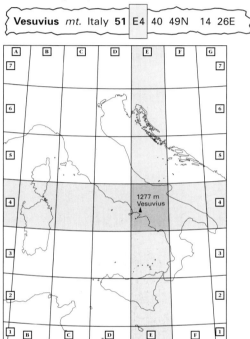

Latitude and longitude

Vesuvius is at latitude 40 49N longitude 14 26E

Vesuvius *mt.* Italy **51** E4 40 49N 14 26E

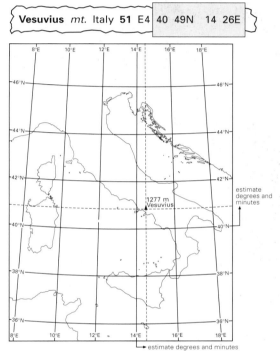

estimate degrees and minutes

→ estimate degrees and minutes

Abbreviations used in the index

admin.	administrative area
b.	bay or harbour
bor.	borough
c.	cape, point or headland
co.	county
est.	estuary
geog.reg.	geographical region
i.	island
is.	islands
l.	lake, lakes, lagoon
mt.	mountain
mts.	mountains
p.	peninsula
pk.	peak
plat.	plateau
pt.	point
r.	river
res.	reservoir
sd.	sound, strait or channel
sum.	summit
tn.	town
u.a.	unitary authority
vol.	volcano

A

Aachen Germany **49** D4 50 46N 6 06E
Aare *r.* Switzerland **49** D2 47 15N 7 30E
Abadan Iran **61** E4 30 20N 48 15E
Abbeville France **48** D5 50 06N 1 51E
Aberaeron Wales **36** C2 52 49N 44 43W
Aberchirder Scotland **31** G2 57 33N 2 38W
Aberconwy and Colwyn *u.a.* Wales **36** D3 53 10N 3 50W
Aberdare Wales **36** D1 51 43N 3 27W
Aberdeen Scotland **31** G2 57 10N 2 04W
Aberdeen City *u.a.* Scotland **31** G2 57 10N 2 00W
Aberdeenshire *u.a.* Scotland **31** G2 57 10N 2 50W
Aberfeldy Scotland **31** F1 56 37N 3 54W
Abergavenny Wales **36** D1 51 50N 3 00W
Abertillery Wales **36** D1 51 45N 3 09W
Aberystwyth Wales **36** C2 52 25N 4 05W
Abha Saudi Arabia **61** E2 18 14N 42 31E
Abidjan Côte d'Ivoire **66** B3 5 19N 4 01W
Abingdon England **38** C2 51 41N 1 17W
Aboyne Scotland **31** G2 57 05N 2 50W
Abu Dhabi United Arab Emirates **61** F3 24 28N 54 25E
Abuja Nigeria **66** C3 9 10N 7 11E
Acapulco Mexico **79** K2 16 51N 99 56W
Accra Ghana **66** B3 5 33N 0 15W
Acklins Island The Bahamas **79** M3 22 30N 74 30W
Aconcagua *mt.* Argentina **85** B4 32 40S 70 02W
Adamawa Highlands Africa **66** D3 7 00N 13 00E
Adana Turkey **43** P3 37 00N 35 19E
Addis Ababa Ethiopia **61** D1 9 03N 38 42E
Adelaide Australia **72** D2 34 55S 138 36E
Aden Yemen Republic **61** E2 12 50N 45 03E
Aden, Gulf of Indian Ocean **61** E2 12 30N 47 30E
Adour *r.* France **48** C1 43 45N 0 30W
Adriatic Sea Mediterranean Sea **51** E5 43 00N 15 00E
Aegean Sea Mediterranean Sea **42** L3 39 00N 24 00E
AFGHANISTAN 58 B4
Agadès Niger **66** C4 17 00N 7 56E
Agadir Morocco **66** B6 30 30N 9 40W
Agra India **58** C3 27 09N 78 00E
Aguascalientes Mexico **79** J3 21 51N 102 18W
Ahaggar *mts.* Algeria **66** C5 23 50N 6 00E

Ahmadabad India **58** C3 23 03N 72 40E
Ahvaz Iran **61** E4 31 17N 48 43E
Ailsa Craig *i.* Scotland **32** D3 55 16N 5 07W
Ain Sefra Algeria **42** F2 32 45N 0 35W
Airdrie Scotland **33** F3 55 52N 3 59W
Aire *r.* England **34** C2 54 00N 2 05W
Aix-en-Provence France **48** F1 43 31N 5 27E
Ajaccio Corsica **51** B4 41 55N 8 43E
Ajdabiya Libya **66** E6 30 46N 20 14E
Akita Japan **59** N2 39 44N 140 05E
Akmola *(Tselinograd)* Kazakhstan **56** H3 51 10N 71 28E
Akureyri Iceland **42** C9 65 41N 18 04W
Alabama *state* U.S.A. **79** L4 32 00N 87 00W
Alaska *state* U.S.A. **78** D7 63 00N 150 00W
Alaska, Gulf of U.S.A. **78** E6 58 00N 147 00W
Alaska Peninsula U.S.A. **78** D6 56 30N 159 00W
Alaska Range *mts.* U.S.A. **78** D7/E7 62 30N 152 30W
Albacete Spain **50** E3 39 00N 1 52W
ALBANIA 42 L4
Albany Australia **72** B2 35 00S 117 53E
Alberta *province* Canada **78** H6 55 00N 115 00W
Ålborg Denmark **42** H7 57 05N 9 50E
Albuquerque U.S.A. **79** J4 35 05N 106 38W
Alcalá de Henares Spain **50** D4 40 28N 3 22W
Alcudia Balearic Islands **50** G3 39 51N 3 06E
Aldabra Islands Indian Ocean **67** E4 9 00S 46 00E
Aldeburgh England **39** F3 52 09N 1 35E
Alderney *i.* Channel Islands British Isles **41** E2 49 43N 2 12W
Aldershot England **38** D2 51 15N 0 47W
Aleppo Syria **61** D4 36 14N 37 10E
Alessándria Italy **51** B6 44 55N 8 37E
Alexandria Egypt **61** C4 31 13N 29 55E
Alexandria Scotland **33** E3 55 59N 4 36W
Algarve *geog. reg.* Portugal **50** A2 37 30N 8 00W
ALGERIA 66 C5
Algiers Algeria **66** C6 36 50N 3 00E
Al Hoceima Morocco **50** D1 35 14N 3 56W
Alicante Spain **50** E3 38 21N 0 29W
Alice Springs Australia **72** D3 23 41S 133 52E
Al Jawf Libya **66** E5 24 12N 23 18E
Allahabad India **58** D3 25 27N 81 50E

Allier *r.* France **48** E3 46 15N 3 15E
Alloa Scotland **33** F4 56 07N 3 49W
Almanzor *mt.* Spain **50** C4 40 15N 5 18W
Almaty Kazakhstan **56** H2 43 19N 76 55E
Almería Spain **50** D2 36 50N 2 26W
Al Mukha Yemen Republic **61** E2 13 20N 43 16E
Aln *r.* England **33** H3 55 30N 1 50W
Alnwick England **33** H3 55 25N 1 42W
Alps *mts.* Europe **49** D2/G2 46 00N 7 30E
Altai Mountains Mongolia **57** K2 47 00N 92 30E
Alton England **38** D2 51 09N 0 59W
Alyth Scotland **31** F1 56 37N 3 13W
Amazon *r.* Brazil **84** D7 2 30S 65 30W
Amble England **33** H3 55 20N 1 34W
Ambleside England **34** C3 54 26N 2 58W
Ambon Indonesia **60** D2 3 41S 128 10E
Amesbury England **38** C2 51 10N 1 47W
Amiens France **48** E4 49 54N 2 18E
Amlwch Wales **36** C3 53 25N 4 20W
Amman Jordan **61** D4 31 04N 46 17E
Ammanford Wales **36** D1 51 48N 3 58W
Amritsar India **58** C4 31 35N 74 56E
Amsterdam Netherlands **49** C5 52 22N 4 54E
Amu Darya *r.* Asia **56** G2 41 00N 61 00E
Amundsen Sea Southern Ocean **86** 72 00S 130 00W
Amur *r.* Asia **57** N3 54 00N 122 00E
Anchorage U.S.A. **78** E7 61 10N 150 00W
Ancona Italy **51** D5 43,37N 13 31E
Andaman Islands India **58** E2 12 00N 94 00E
Andaman Sea Indian Ocean **58** E2 13 00N 95 00E
Andes *mts.* South America **84/85** B8/C5 10 00S 77 00W
Andizhan Uzbekistan **56** H2 40 40N 72 12E
ANDORRA 50 F5
Andover England **38** C2 51 13N 1 28W
Andros *i.* The Bahamas **79** M3 24 00N 78 00W
Aneto *mt.* Spain **50** F5 42 37N 0 40E
Angara *r.* Russia **57** K3 59 00N 97 00E
Angeles The Philippines **60** D4 15 09N 120 33E
Angers France **48** C3 47 29N 0 32W
Anglesey *u.a.* Wales **36** C3 53 18N 4 25W
ANGOLA 67 B3
Angoulême France **48** D2 45 40N 0 10E
Anguilla *i.* Leeward Islands **79** N2 18 14N 63 05W

Angus *u.a.* Scotland **31** F1/G1 56 45N 3 00W
Ankara Turkey **43** N3 39 55N 32 50E
'Annaba Algeria **66** C6 36 55N 7 47E
An Najaf Iraq **61** E4 31 59N 44 19E
Annam Range *mts.* Laos/Vietnam **60** B4 19 00N 104 00E
Annan Scotland **33** F2 54 59N 3 16W
Annan *r.* Scotland **33** F3 55 05N 3 20W
Annapurna *mt.* Nepal **58** D3 28 34N 83 50E
Annecy France **48** G2 45 54N 6 07E
Anshan China **59** D4 41 05N 122 58E
Anstruther Scotland **33** G4 56 14N 2 42W
Antalya Turkey **43** N3 36 53N 30 42E
Antananarivo Madagascar **67** E3 18 52S 47 30E
Antarctic Peninsula Antarctica **86** 68 00S 65 00W
Antibes France **48** G1 43 35N 7 07E
Antigua *i.* Antigua & Barbuda **84** C9 17 09N 61 49W
ANTIGUA AND BARBUDA 79 N2
Antofagasta Chile **84** B5 23 40S 70 23W
Antrim Northern Ireland **32** C2 54 43N 6 13W
Antrim *district* Northern Ireland **32** C2 54 45N 6 25W
Antrim Mountains Northern Ireland **32** C3/D2 55 00N 6 10W
Antwerp Belgium **49** C4 51 13N 4 25E
Anxi China **59** A5 40 32N 95 57E
Aomori Japan **59** N3 40 50N 140 43E
Aosta Italy **51** A6 45 43N 7 19E
Aparri The Philippines **60** D4 18 22N 121 40E
Apeldoorn Netherlands **49** C5 52 13N 5 57E
Appalachians *mts.* U.S.A. **79** L4 37 00N 82 00W
Appennines *mts.* Italy **51** C6/F4 44 30N 10 00E
Appleby-in-Westmorland England **34** C3 53 36N 2 29W
Aqaba Jordan **61** D3 29 32N 35 00E
Arabian Sea Indian Ocean **7** 17 00N 60 00E
Aracaju Brazil **84** F6 10 54S 37 07W
Arad Romania **42** L5 46 10N 21 19E
Arafura Sea Australia **72** D5 9 00S 133 00E
Araguaia *r.* Brazil **84** D6 12 30S 51 00W
Arak Iran **61** E4 34 05N 49 42E
Araks *r.* Asia **61** E4 39 30N 48 00E
Aral Sea Asia **56** G2 45 00N 60 00E
Aran Fawddy *mt.* Wales **36** D2 52 47N 3 41W

Kobe Japan 59 M1 34 40N 135 12E
Koblenz Germany 49 D4 50 21N 7 36E
Kochi Japan 59 L1 33 33N 133 32E
Kodiak Island U.S.A. 78 D6 57 20N 153 40W
Kokand Uzbekistan 56 H2 40 33N 70 55E
Kolhapur India 58 C2 16 40N 74 20E
Kolyma r. Russia 57 R4 68 00N 152 00E
Komsomolsk-on-Amur Russia 57 P3 50 32N 136 59E
Konya Turkey 43 N3 37 51N 32 30E
Koriyama Japan 59 N2 37 23N 140 22E
Kosciusko, Mount Australia 72 E2 36 27S 148 17E
Košice Slovakia 42 L5 48 44N 21 15E
Kota Baharu Malaysia 60 B3 6 08N 102 14E
Kota Kinabalu Malaysia 60 C3 5 59N 116 04E
Kotlas Russia 43 R8 61 15N 46 35E
Kragujevac Serbia Yugoslavia 42 L4 44 01N 20 55E
Kra, Isthmus of Myanmar/Thailand 60 A4 10 20N 99 00E
Kranj Slovenia 51 E7 46 15N 14 20E
Krasnodar Russia 56 D2 45 02N 39 00E
Krasnovodsk Turkmenistan 56 F2 40 01N 53 00E
Krasnoyarsk Russia 57 K3 56 05N 92 46E
Kratie Cambodia 60 B4 12 30N 106 03E
Krefeld Germany 49 D4 51 20N 6 32E
Kremenchuk Ukraine 43 N5 49 03N 33 25E
Krishna r. India 58 C2 16 00N 79 00E
Krivoy Rog see Kryvy Rih
Krung Thep see Bangkok
Kryvy Rih (Krivoy Rog) Ukraine 56 D2 47 55N 33 24E
Kuala Lumpur Malaysia 60 B3 3 09N 101 42E
Kuala Terengganu Malaysia 60 B3 5 20N 103 09E
Kuantan Malaysia 60 B3 3 48N 103 19E
Kuching Malaysia 60 C3 1 35N 110 21E
Kuh-e-Hazaran mt. Iran 61 F3 29 35N 57 20E
Kumamoto Japan 59 L1 32 50N 130 42E
Kumasi Ghana 66 B3 6 45N 1 35W
Kunlun Shan mts. China 58 D4 36 30N 85 00E
Kunming China 59 B2 25 04N 102 41E
Kupang Indonesia 60 D1 10 13S 123 38E
Kurgan Russia 56 G3 55 30N 65 20E
Kuril Islands Russia 57 R2 50 00N 155 00E
Kursk Russia 56 D3 51 45N 36 14E
Kushiro Japan 59 N3 42 58N 144 24E
Kutaisi Georgia 43 Q4 42 15N 42 44E
KUWAIT 61 E3
Kuwait Kuwait 61 E3 29 20N 48 00E
Kuybyshev see Samara
Kwangju South Korea 59 D3 35 07N 126 52E
Kyle of Lochalsh Scotland 30 D2 57 17N 5 43W
Kyoga, Lake Uganda 67 D5 2 00N 34 00E
Kyoto Japan 59 M2 35 02N 135 45E
Kyushu i. Japan 59 L1 32 20N 131 00E

L

Laccadive Islands see Lakshadweep
La Coruña Spain 50 A5 43 22N 8 24W
Ladoga, Lake Russia 56 D4 61 00N 30 00E
Lae Papua New Guinea 72 E5 6 45S 147 00E
Lagos Nigeria 66 C3 6 27N 3 28E
La Grande Rivière r. Canada 78 L6 53 34N 74 36W
Lahore Pakistan 58 C4 31 35N 74 18E
Lairg Scotland 31 E3 58 01N 4 25W
Lake District geog. reg. England 34 B3/C3 54 30N 3 00W
Lakshadweep (Laccadive Islands) India 58 C2 9 30N 73 00E
Lambert Glacier Antarctica 86 73 00S 70 00E
Lambourn r. England 38 C2 51 30N 1 30W
Lammermuir Hills Scotland 33 G3 55 50N 2 45W
Lampedusa i. Italy 51 D1 35 00N 12 00E
Lampeter Wales 36 C2 52 07N 4 05W
Lanark Scotland 33 F3 55 41N 3 48W
Lancang Jiang (Mekong) r. China/Myanmar/Laos/Cambodia 59 A3 32 00N 98 00E
Lancashire co. England 34 C2 53 50N 2 30W
Lancaster England 34 C3 54 03N 2 48W
Land's End c. England 40 B3 50 03N 5 44W
Langholm Scotland 33 G3 55 09N 3 00W
Languedoc geog. reg. France 48 E1/F2 44 00N 4 00E
Lanzhou China 59 B3 36 01N 103 45E
LAOS 60 B4
La Paz Bolivia 84 C6 16 30S 68 10W
La Plata Argentina 85 D4 34 52S 57 55W
La Puebla Balearic Islands 50 G3 39 46N 3 01E
Largs Scotland 32 E3 55 48N 4 52W
Lárisa Greece 42 L3 39 38N 22 25E
Larne Northern Ireland 32 D2 54 51N 5 49W
Larne district Northern Ireland 32 D2 54 50N 5 50W
La Rochelle France 48 C3 46 10N 1 10W
Larsen Ice Shelf Antarctica 86 67 00S 62 00W
La Sagra mt. Spain 50 D2 37 57N 2 34W
Las Palmas Canary Islands 66 A5 28 08N 15 27W
La Spezia Italy 51 B6 44 07N 9 48E
Las Vegas U.S.A. 79 H4 36 10N 115 10W
Latakia Syria 61 D4 35 31N 35 47E
Latina Italy 51 D4 41 28N 12 53E
LATVIA 42 M7
Launceston Australia 72 E1 41 27S 147 09E
Launceston England 40 C3 50 38N 4 21W
Laurencekirk Scotland 31 G1 56 50N 2 29W
Lausanne Switzerland 49 D2 46 32N 6 39E
Laval France 48 C4 48 04N 0 45W
Leader Water r. Scotland 33 G3 55 45N 2 50W
LEBANON 61 D4
Ledbury England 37 E2 52 02N 2 25W
Leeds England 34 D2 53 50N 1 35W
Leeuwin, Cape Australia 72 B2 34 21S 115 08E
le Havre France 48 D4 49 30N 0 06E
Leicester England 37 F2 52 38N 1 05W
Leicestershire co. England 37 F2/G2 52 30N 1 00W
Leiden Netherlands 49 C5 52 10N 4 30E
Leighton Buzzard England 38 D2 51 55N 0 41W
Leipzig Germany 49 G4 51 20N 12 25E
Leith Hill England 38 D2 51 11N 0 23W
Leitrim co. Republic of Ireland 32 A2 54 05N 8 00W
le Mans France 48 D4 48 00N 0 12E
Lena r. Russia 57 N4 64 30N 127 00E
Leningrad see St. Petersburg
Lens France 48 E5 50 26N 2 50E
Leominster England 37 E2 52 14N 2 45W
León Mexico 79 J3 21 10N 101 42W
León Spain 50 C5 42 35N 5 34W
Le Puy France 48 E2 45 03N 3 53E
Lérida Spain 50 F4 41 37N 0 38E
Lerwick Scotland 29 D3 60 09N 1 09W
LESOTHO 67 C2
Lessay France 41 F2 49 13N 1 32W
Lesser Antilles is. West Indies 79 N2 18 00N 65 00W
Letchworth England 38 D2 51 58N 0 14W
le Touquet-Paris-Plage France 39 F1 50 13N 1 36E
Letterkenny Donegal Republic of Ireland 32 B2 54 57N 7 44W
Leverkusen Germany 49 D4 51 02N 6 59E
Levin New Zealand 73 D2 40 37S 175 17E
Lewes England 38 E1 50 52N 0 01E
Lewis i. Scotland 30 C3 58 15N 6 30W
Leyburn England 34 D3 54 19N 1 49W
Leyland England 34 C2 53 42N 2 42W
Leyte i. The Philippines 60 D4 11 00N 125 00E
Lhasa China 58 E3 29 08N 87 43E
Lianyungang China 59 C3 34 37N 119 10E
Liao He r. China 59 D4 42 30N 122 00E
Liard r. Canada 78 G7 61 00N 122 00W
LIBERIA 66 B3
Libreville Gabon 66 C3 0 30N 9 25E
LIBYA 66 D5
Libyan Desert North Africa 61 C3 25 00N 25 00E
Lichfield England 37 F2 52 42N 1 48W
Liddel Water r. England/Scotland 33 G3 55 15N 2 50W
LIECHTENSTEIN 49 E2
Liège Belgium 49 C4 50 38N 5 35E
Liepāja Latvia 42 L7 56 30N 21 00E
Likasi Zaïre 67 C3 10 58S 26 47E
Lille France 48 E5 50 39N 3 05E
Lillers France 39 G1 50 34N 2 29E
Lilongwe Malawi 67 D3 13 58S 33 49E
Lima Peru 84 B6 12 06S 8 40W
Limassol Cyprus 43 N2 34 04N 33 03E
Limavady Northern Ireland 32 C3 55 03N 6 57W
Limavady district Northern Ireland 32 B2/C2 54 50N 7 00W
Limoges France 48 D2 45 50N 1 15E
Limpopo r. Southern Africa 67 C2 22 30S 28 00E
Lincoln England 35 E2 53 14N 0 33W
Lincolnshire co. England 35 E2 53 10N 0 20W
Lincoln Wolds hills England 35 E2 53 25N 0 05W
Lingga i. Indonesia 60 B2 0 10S 104 40E
Linköping Sweden 42 K7 58 25N 15 35E
Linlithgow Scotland 33 F3 55 59N 3 37W
Linz Austria 42 J5 48 19N 14 18E
Lipetsk Russia 56 D3 52 37N 39 36E
Lisbon Portugal 50 A3 38 44N 9 08W
Lisburn Northern Ireland 32 C2 54 31N 6 03W
Lisburn district Northern Ireland 32 C2 54 30N 6 10W
Lisieux France 48 D4 49 09N 0 14E
Liskeard England 40 C3 50 28N 4 28W
Lismore i. Scotland 30 D1 56 30N 5 30W
LITHUANIA 42 L7
Littlehampton England 38 D1 50 48N 0 33W
Little Minch sd. Scotland 30 C2 57 45N 6 30W
Little Ouse r. England 39 E3 52 30N 0 30E
Little Rock U.S.A. 79 K4 34 42N 92 17W
Liuzhou China 59 B2 24 17N 109 15E
Liverpool England 34 C2 53 25N 2 55W
Livingston Scotland 33 F3 55 53N 3 32W
Livorno Italy 51 C5 43 33N 10 18E
Lizard England 40 B2 49 57N 5 13W
Lizard Point England 40 B2 49 56N 5 13W
Ljubljana Slovenia 51 E7 46 04N 14 30E
Llandeilo Wales 36 D1 51 53N 3 59W
Llandovery Wales 36 D1 51 59N 3 48W
Llandrindod Wells Wales 36 D2 52 15N 3 23W
Llandudno Wales 36 D3 53 19N 3 49W
Llanelli Wales 36 C1 51 42N 4 10W
Llangollen Wales 36 D2 52 58N 3 10W
Llanidloes Wales 36 D2 52 27N 3 32W
Lleyn Peninsula Wales 36 C2 52 53N 4 30W
Lobito Angola 67 B3 12 20S 13 34E
Lochaline tn. Scotland 30 D1 56 32N 5 47W
Loch Arkaig l. Scotland 30 D1 56 59N 5 10W
Loch Awe l. Scotland 30/31 D1 56 15N 5 17W
Lochdon tn. Scotland 30 D1 56 25N 5 35W
Loch Doon l. Scotland 33 E3 55 26N 4 38W
Loch Earn l. Scotland 31 E1 56 25N 4 10W
Loch Eishort est. Scotland 30 D2 57 08N 6 00W
Loch Eriboll b. Scotland 31 E3 58 31N 4 41W
Loch Ericht l. Scotland 31 E1 56 48N 4 25W
Loch Etive l. Scotland 30/31 D1 56 30N 5 10W
Loch Fyne b. Scotland 32 D4 56 10N 5 05W
Lochgilphead tn. Scotland 32 D4 56 03N 5 26W
Loch Katrine l. Scotland 33 E4 56 16N 4 30W
Loch Ken l. Scotland 33 E3 55 02N 4 07W
Loch Leven l. Scotland 31 F1 56 15N 3 23W
Loch Linnhe b. Scotland 30 D1 56 35N 5 25W
Loch Lochy l. Scotland 31 E1 56 58N 4 55W
Loch Lomond l. Scotland 33 E4 56 10N 4 35W
Loch Long l. Scotland 32/33 E4 56 10N 4 50W
Lochmaben tn. Scotland 33 F3 55 08N 3 27W
Lochmaddy tn. Scotland 30 B2 57 36N 7 08W
Loch Nan Clar l. Scotland 31 E3 58 30N 4 00W
Loch Maree l. Scotland 30 D2 57 40N 5 30W
Loch Mullardoch l. Scotland 31 E2 57 27N 4 58W
Lochnagar mt. Scotland 31 F1 56 57N 3 16W
Loch Ness l. Scotland 31 E2 57 02N 4 30W
Loch Rannoch l. Scotland 31 E1 56 41N 4 18W
Lochranza tn. Scotland 32 D3 55 42N 5 18W
Loch Shiel l. Scotland 30 D1 56 45N 5 35W
Loch Shin l. Scotland 31 E3 58 05N 4 30W
Loch Snizort b. Scotland 30 C2 57 30N 6 30W
Loch Tay l. Scotland 31 E1 56 31N 4 10W
Loch Torridon b. Scotland 30 D2 57 35N 5 46W
Lockerbie Scotland 33 F3 55 07N 3 22W
Łódź Poland 42 K6 51 49N 19 28E
Logan, Mount Canada 78 E7 60 34N 140 25W
Logroño Spain 50 D5 42 28N 2 26W
Loire r. France 48 D3 47 30N 1 00E
Lolland i. Denmark 49 F6 54 45N 12 20E
Lombok i. Indonesia 60 C2 8 30S 116 30E
Lomé Togo 66 C3 6 10N 1 21E
London England 38 D2 51 30N 0 10W
Londonderry Northern Ireland 32 B2 54 59N 7 19W
Londonderry district Northern Ireland 32 B2 54 55N 7 20W
Londrina Brazil 84 D5 23 18S 51 13W
Long Eaton England 37 F2 52 54N 1 15W
Long Island The Bahamas 79 M3 23 20N 75 00W
Long Mynd sum. England 37 E2 52 32N 2 52W
Longreach Australia 72 E3 23 26S 144 15E
Longs Peak U.S.A. 79 J5 40 20N 105 50W
Looe England 40 C3 51 21N 4 27W
Lorient France 48 B3 47 45N 3 21W
Los Angeles U.S.A. 79 H4 34 00N 118 15W
Lossiemouth Scotland 31 F2 57 43N 3 18W
Lostwithiel England 40 C3 50 25N 4 40W
Lot r. France 48 E2 44 30N 2 15E
Lough Allen l. Republic of Ireland 32 A2 54 15N 8 00W
Lough Beg l. Northern Ireland 32 C2 54 48N 6 16W
Loughborough England 37 F2 52 47N 1 11W
Lough Derg l. Republic of Ireland 32 B2 52 55N 8 15W
Lough Foyle est. Northern Ireland/Republic of Ireland 32 B3 55 10N 7 10W
Lough Macnean Lower l. Northern Ireland 32 B2 54 17N 7 50W
Lough Macnean Upper l. Northern Ireland/Republic of Ireland 32 B2 54 18N 7 55W
Lough Melvin l. Northern Ireland/Republic of Ireland 32 A2 54 25N 8 05W
Lough Neagh l. Northern Ireland 32 C2 54 35N 6 30W
Lough Oughter l. Republic of Ireland 32 B2 54 00N 7 30W
Lough Swilly b. Republic of Ireland 32 B3 55 20N 7 35W
Louisiana state U.S.A. 79 K4 32 00N 92 00W
Louisville U.S.A. 79 L4 38 13N 85 48W
Lourdes France 48 C1 43 06N 0 02W
Louth England 35 E2 53 22N 0 01W
Louth co. Republic of Ireland 32 C1/2 53 55N 6 25W
Lower California p. Mexico 79 H3 27 30N 113 00W
Lower Lough Erne l. Northern Ireland 32 B2 54 25N 7 45W
Lowestoft England 39 F3 52 29N 1 45E
Lowther Hills Scotland 33 F3 55 25N 3 45W
Lualaba r. Zaïre 67 C4 4 00S 26 30E
Luanda Angola 67 B4 8 50S 13 15E
Luang Prabang Laos 60 B4 19 53N 102 10E
Lubango Angola 67 B3 14 55S 13 30E
Lübeck Germany 49 F5 53 52N 10 40E
Lublin Poland 42 L6 51 18N 22 31E
Lubumbashi Zaïre 67 C3 11 41S 27 29E
Luce Bay Scotland 32/33 E2 54 47N 4 50W
Lucerne Switzerland 49 E2 47 03N 8 17E
Lucknow India 58 D3 26 50N 80 54E
Lüderitz Namibia 67 B2 26 38S 15 10E
Ludhiana India 58 C4 30 56N 75 52E
Ludlow England 37 E2 52 22N 2 43W
Ludwigshafen Germany 49 E3 49 29N 8 27E
Lugano Switzerland 49 E2 46 01N 8 57E
Luhans'k Ukraine 56 D2 48 35N 39 20E
Luleå Sweden 42 L9 65 35N 22 10E
Lundy i. England 40 C4 51 11N 4 40W
Lune r. England 34 C3 54 15N 2 40W
Luoyang China 59 C3 34 47N 112 26E
Lurgan Northern Ireland 32 C2 54 28N 6 20W
Lusaka Zambia 67 C3 15 26S 28 20E
Luton England 38 D2 51 53N 0 25W
LUXEMBOURG 49 C3/D3
Luxembourg Luxembourg 49 D3 49 37N 6 08E
Luxor Egypt 61 D3 25 41N 32 24E
Luzon i. The Philippines 60 D4 15 00N 122 00E
L'viv Ukraine 56 C2 49 50N 24 00E
Lybster Scotland 31 F3 58 18N 3 13W
Lyme Bay England 41 E3 50 40N 2 55W
Lyme Regis England 41 E3 50 44N 2 57W
Lymington England 38 C1 50 46N 1 33W
Lynn Lake tn. Canada 78 J6 56 51N 101 01W
Lynton England 40 D4 51 15N 3 50W
Lyons France 48 F2 45 46N 4 50E
Lys r. France 39 G1 50 40N 2 10E
Lytham St. Anne's England 34 B2 53 45N 3 01W

M

Maas r. Netherlands 49 C4 51 50N 5 45E
Maastricht Netherlands 49 C4 50 51N 5 42E
Mablethorpe England 35 F2 53 21N 0 15E
Macao territory Portugal 59 C2 22 10N 113 40E
Macapá Brazil 84 D8 0 04N 51 04W
Macclesfield England 34 C2 53 16N 2 07W
Macdonnell Ranges Australia 72 D3 23 42S 128 42E
Macduff Scotland 31 G2 57 40N 2 30W
MACEDONIA, FORMER YUGOSLAV REPUBLIC OF (FYROM) 42 L4
Maceió Brazil 84 F7 9 40S 35 44W
Machynlleth Wales 36 D2 52 35N 3 51W
Mackay, Lake Australia 72 C3 22 25S 128 42E
Mackenzie r. Canada 78 G7 64 00N 123 00W
Mackenzie Mountains Canada 78 G7 66 00N 132 00W
McKinley, Mount U.S.A. 78 E7 62 02N 151 01W
Mâcon France 48 F3 46 18N 4 50E
MADAGASCAR 67 E2/3
Madang Papua New Guinea 72 E5 5 14S 145 45E
Madeira r. Brazil 84 C7 6 00S 61 30W
Madeira Islands Atlantic Ocean 5 32 45N 17 00W
Madras India 58 D2 13 05N 80 18E
Madrid Spain 50 D4 40 25N 3 43W
Madura i. Indonesia 60 C2 7 00S 113 00E
Madurai India 58 C1 9 55N 78 07E
Maebashi Japan 59 M2 36 24N 139 04E
Magadan Russia 57 R3 59 38N 150 50E
Magdalena r. Colombia 84 B8 3 00N 75 40W
Magdeburg Germany 49 F5 52 08N 11 37E
Maggiore, Lake Italy 51 B6/7 46 00N 8 00E
Maghera Northern Ireland 32 C2 54 51N 6 40W
Magherafelt Northern Ireland 32 C2 54 45N 6 36W
Magherafelt district Northern Ireland 32 C2 54 45N 6 50W
Magnitogorsk Russia 56 F3 53 28N 59 06E
Mahajanga Madagascar 67 E3 15 40S 46 20E
Mahakam r. Indonesia 60 C3 0 30N 116 00E
Mahilyow (Mogilev) Belarus 56 D3 53 54N 30 20E
Mahón Balearic Islands 50 H3 39 54N 4 15E
Maidenhead England 38 D2 51 32N 0 44W
Maidstone England 39 E2 51 17N 0 32E
Maiduguri Nigeria 66 D4 11 53N 13 16E
Main r. Germany 49 F4 50 00N 10 30E
Main r. Northern Ireland 32 C2 54 50N 6 25W
Mai-Ndombe, Lake Zaïre 67 B4 2 00S 18 20E
Maine state U.S.A. 79 N5 45 00N 70 00W
Mainland i. Orkney Islands Scotland 29 B1/B2 59 00N 3 15W
Mainland i. Shetland Islands Scotland 29 D3 60 15N 1 20W
Mainz Germany 49 D3 50 00N 8 16E
Majorca i. Balearic Islands 50 G3 39 50N 2 30E
Makassar Strait Indonesia 60 C2 0 00 119 00E
Makeyevka Ukraine 56 D2 48 01N 38 00E
Makhachkala Russia 56 E2 42 59N 47 30E
Malabo Equatorial Guinea 66 C3 3 45N 8 48E
Malacca, Strait of Indonesia 60 B3 4 00N 100 00E
Málaga Spain 50 C2 36 43N 4 25W
Malahide Dublin Republic of Ireland 36 A3 53 27N 6 09W
Malakal Sudan 61 D1 9 31N 31 40E
Malang Indonesia 60 C2 7 59S 112 45E
Malanje Angola 67 B4 9 32S 16 20E
Malatya Turkey 43 P3 38 22N 38 18E
MALAWI 67 D3
Malawi, Lake see Nyasa, Lake
Malaya admin. Malaysia 60 B3 5 00N 102 00E
MALAYSIA 60 B3/C3
MALDIVES 58 C1
MALI 66 B4
Malin Head c. Republic of Ireland 32 B3 55 30N 7 20W
Mallaig Scotland 30 D2 57 00N 5 50W
Malmesbury England 38 B2 51 36N 2 06W
Malmö Sweden 42 J7 55 35N 13 00E
MALTA 51 E1
Malton England 35 E3 54 08N 0 48W
Manacor Balearic Islands 50 G3 39 35N 3 12E
Manado Indonesia 60 D3 1 32N 124 55E
Managua Nicaragua 79 L2 12 06N 86 18W
Manaus Brazil 84 D7 3 06S 60 00W
Manawatu r. New Zealand 73 D2 40 30S 176 00E
Manchester England 34 C2 53 30N 2 15W
Mandalay Myanmar 58 E3 21 57N 96 04E
Manfredonia Italy 51 E4 41 37N 15 55E
Mangalore India 58 C2 12 54N 74 51E
Mangotsfield England 38 B2 51 29N 2 31W
Manila The Philippines 60 D4 14 37N 120 58E
Manitoba province Canada 78 K6 55 00N 98 00W
Manizales Colombia 84 B8 5 03N 75 32W
Mannheim Germany 49 E3 49 30N 8 28E
Mansfield England 37 F3 53 09N 1 11W
Manzanares Spain 50 D3 39 00N 3 23W
Maputo Mozambique 67 D2 25 58S 32 35E
Maracaibo Venezuela 84 B9 10 44N 71 37W
Maracaibo, Lake Venezuela 84 B8 9 50N 71 30W
Marañon r. Peru 84 B7 7 00S 77 40W
Marbella Spain 50 C2 36 31N 4 53W
Marble Bar Australia 72 B3 21 10S 119 43E
Mar del Plata Argentina 85 D4 38 00S 57 32W
Marden England 39 E2 51 11N 0 30E
Margarita i. Venezuela 79 N2 11 30N 64 00W
Margate England 39 F2 51 24N 1 24E
Maribor Slovenia 51 E7 46 34N 15 38E
Marie Byrd Land geog. reg. Antarctica 86 77 00S 130 00W
Mariscal Estigarribia Paraguay 84 C5 22 03S 60 35W
Mariupol Ukraine 56 D2 47 05N 37 34E
Market Drayton England 37 E2 52 54N 2 29W
Market Harborough England 37 G2 52 29N 0 55W
Market Rasen England 35 E2 53 24N 0 21W
Markham, Mount Antarctica 86 82 45S 160 25E
Marlborough England 38 C2 51 26N 1 43W
Marlow England 38 D2 51 35N 0 48W
Marne r. France 48 E4 49 00N 4 00E
Marrakesh Morocco 66 B6 31 49N 8 00W
Marsala Italy 51 D2 37 48N 12 27E
Marseille France 48 F1 43 18N 5 22E
MARSHALL ISLANDS 5
Martinique i. Lesser Antilles 79 N2 14 30N 61 00W
Maryborough Australia 72 F3 25 33S 152 42E
Maryland state U.S.A. 79 M4 39 00N 77 00W
Maryport England 34 B3 54 43N 3 30W
Maseru Lesotho 67 C2 29 19S 27 29E
Mashhad Iran 61 F4 36 16N 59 34E
Massachusetts state U.S.A. 79 M5 42 00N 72 00W
Massawa Eritrea 61 D2 15 42N 39 25E
Massif Central mts. France 48 E2 45 00N 3 30E
Masterton New Zealand 73 D2 40 57S 175 39E
Matadi Zaïre 67 B4 5 50S 13 32E
Matamoros Mexico 79 K3 25 33N 103 51W
Matlock England 37 F3 53 08N 1 32W
Mato Grosso geog. reg. Brazil 84 D6 14 00S 56 00W
Matsue Japan 59 L2 35 29N 133 04E
Matsuyama Japan 59 L1 33 50N 132 47E
Matterhorn mt. Switzerland 49 D1 45 59N 7 39E
MAURITANIA 66 A5
MAURITIUS 5
Maybole Scotland 33 E3 55 21N 4 41W
Maykop Russia 43 Q4 44 37N 40 48E
Mazatlán Mexico 79 J3 23 11N 106 25W
Mbandaka Zaïre 67 B5 0 03N 18 28E
Mbuji-Mayi Zaïre 67 C4 6 10S 23 39E
Mecca Saudi Arabia 61 D3 21 26N 39 49E
Medan Indonesia 60 A3 3 35N 98 39E
Medellín Colombia 84 B8 6 15N 75 36W
Medina Saudi Arabia 61 D3 24 30N 39 35E
Mediterranean Sea Africa/Europe 42/43 35 00N 15 00E
Medway r. England 39 E2 51 24N 0 30E
Meekatharra Australia 72 B3 26 35S 118 30E
Meerut India 58 C3 29 00N 77 42E
Mega Ethiopia 61 D1 4 02N 38 19E
Meharry, Mount Australia 72 B3 22 58S 118 35E
Meig r. Scotland 31 E2 57 40N 4 50W
Meknes Morocco 66 B6 33 53N 5 37W
Mekong (Lancang Jiang) r. Cambodia/Laos/Myanmar/China 59 B1 15 00N 105 00E
Melbourne Australia 72 E2 37 49S 144 58E